The Definitive Guide

To Exam Revision

... Making Revision FUN Using The MASSIVE Goal Principle

by David Hyner PSAE FPSA ABNLP ALAM

www.davidhyner.com

www.stretchdevelopment.com

The content of this book gives students the skills and confidence to achieve their exam goals and is intended as a guide to motivate those revising for exams of any sort to raise their aspirations and levels of attainment.

It is the culmination of years of research interviews with top achievers and over 15 years work in the education sector presenting talks and workshops to between 10'000 – 50'000 students and education professionals every year across the UK and around the world.

Students should always assess what is "right" for them to be doing, and what is fair to both themselves and those around them before embarking upon their massive goals. It is too tempting to do what seems easy or the "right things" in the moment to makes us feel better about ourselves, when it is nearly always better, even if it is "harder to do", to do the "RIGHT THING".

Thanks to all of the amazing young adults I meet each year who have had the courage to go and find out what they are truly capable of achieving...... you guys ROCK and continually inspire me beyond words!

About the author:

David Hyner psae fpsa abnlp alam

www.davidhyner.com
www.stretchdevelopment.com

David has worked in schools, colleges and universities all over the UK and the world giving keynote talks and workshops to between 10,000 and 50,000 students, parents and teachers each year.

In that time he has seen, worked with and helped thousands of students who had given up on themselves (or others had given up on them) turn their results and in some cases their lives around and achieve BIG (MASSIVE) goals !. David is a renowned professional speaker and in this book he gives you the knowledge, skills and confidence to set and achieve your MASSIVE exam goals;

and ....how **others just like you, have done the same.**

This book gives you simple, easy to apply, effective solutions to improved self management and goal setting be it for personal goals or education/learning goals. It's based on many years of research into how highly effective top achievers set and achieve goals.

This gives you increased confidence, certainty and conviction to be the young adult that is talked about… for all the right reasons.

David delivers workshops and talks on the subject of personal effectiveness including:

Independent learning, Goal Setting, Confidence, Memory Skills, Revision Skills, Motivation, Presentation Skills, Enterprise Events, Aim-Higher, Attitude, Adventures, Communications, Emotional Intelligence, Gifted & Talented, Interview Skills, Fundraising, Team Building, Stress Prevention, Body Language, Personal Responsibility, … and more.

The tips and advice given within these pages are not guaranteed to work for everyone as everyone has their own work ethic and unique style of working.

They are, however, based upon tried and tested techniques that David and the contributors have seen used by successful and effective students and teachers, and/or used by them to improve motivation and raise attainment.

Introduction.

Welcome to

The Definitive Guide To Exam Revision

Making Revision **FUN**

Using The MASSIVE Goal Principle.

My name is David Hyner from

www.stretchdevelopment.com

(www.davidhyner.com)

I am a researcher and professional speaker that has found out how the super successful people in the world go about setting and achieving their goals and seemingly appear so much more effective than the rest of us.

Over many years I've travelled around the world and interviewed face to face and over the telephone men and women who have achieved at the highest level.

It has been my privilege and honour to have interviewed top achievers from sport, world champions, Olympic gold medallists, world record holders.

I've interviewed scientists, entrepreneurs and captains of industry. I have even interviewed memory champions and academic experts to understand how successful people in the world of "learning" think and behave.

I have also interviewed the multi-millionaires of this world. Inventors, explorers, entertainers, authors; basically anyone I could find who has achieved with integrity at the very highest level.

The real gold though in relation to exams is what I learnt from interviewing and working alongside memory masters, world champion mind-mappers, neuro-scientists and psychologists who had studied or work on the memory and recall mechanisms of the brain.

The reason I did this is so that you don't have to.

I found out how these people think and behave when they go about setting and achieving their goals.

So… If you use what is explained within the pages of this short book I challenge you to not become more effective (as a minimum) and possibly achieve your big goal as a consequence…. But you must **take action**.

What you're going to get in this book is the ability to get inside the minds of top achievers because what we discovered is that top achievers think and behave differently. They are not extraordinary people … but in fact they are ordinary people like you and I who happen to just think and behave differently.

That is it!

Our thoughts and behaviours will determine our outcomes and top achievers think and behave differently, however you can do the same as they do.

What I'm going to share with you in this book is how they think and behave so that you can do the same. And I promise you … it's easy.

So, how can you, and how should you be using this goal setting book?

The first time you read the book, literally, just read it allowing the words to sink in without any pressure to understand or use any of it.

The second time you read it I want you to make notes. I want you to get some paper, some large pieces of paper if possible, some coloured pens and have your diary to hand as well. The second time you read it make notes, lots and lots of notes.

Anything you read that is of, at all, any relevance to you. Use coloured pens, note any great quotes, doodle, draw images. Make them colourful and vibrant so that your brain is attracted to them. The diary? Well, I'll go into that later on.

The third time you read the book, I will ask you to be creating your pyramid. By pyramid, I mean the structure around which we set and achieve goals based upon what top achievers have taught us. And I will be asking you to create your own pyramid to work on your own goal.

The fourth time you read is purely as a reminder. The more times you read this book and refer to this, the more likely you are to use it. I suggest you read it as many times as possible, but four as a minimum.

So....

- First time - read.
- Second time – make notes.
- Third time – actually create your goal.
- Fourth time – just to remind yourself.

You may be thinking, well, top achievers they set goals, ok, they're top achievers.

Of course they do. I'm not a top achiever, I can't set goals. Well, you know what, everybody is a human being. All you need to do is to think and behave differently to get better results. This book will show you HOW.

At the age of 30 I had …well, at best, an average life. The only two things I could claim of any significance to have achieved was to have started my own business and found my beautiful wife who was crazy enough to love me and marry me. Apart from that, well, most of my life goals and ambitions were as yet to be achieved … or even started. When I was told by my teachers to expect C & D grades… I believed them, and as if by magic, have a guess what grades I got? Talk about a self fulfilling prophecy eh? As a result I tended to believe that I was not cut out for learning and was not that clever.

What did I do?

I used the information that you're about to experience and **it changed my life for ever** … for the better.

I went to night school one night a week at a local further education college where, using the techniques enclosed in these pages I got a set of qualifications inside three years that would normally have taken twice that time… and with pretty amazing grades as well.

My wife (then a student) was told at school that she was average and was "not clever enough to go to University !!!"

WHAT ??

Using these techniques she did NOT get "a" degree… but instead got a teaching degree, followed by a dietetic degree followed by a masters degree in Autism studies, and is now considering if she should do a doctorate. Not clever enough eh? Lol

I took it into companies, into schools, I now also take it into colleges, universities and local authorities and I help people to set and achieve their goals. But I did this only after I had used it to start and begin to achieve my own goals as for me I wanted to have some credibility on the subject if I was to share it with others and make any difference. I have used it in personal goals, in charity fundraising goals, in my business and in my personal life. You can do the same.

What is your goal? Is it an examination related goal or maybe a personal goal? A life dream or ambition? Is it a charitable goal? Maybe you want to be more philanthropic, help other people. Or maybe it's a business goal. Maybe you need to get better grades or change your attitude? Maybe you need to boost your CV, learn an instrument or do some community work? Either way, you determine what you use it for. **But please … use it.**

Section One

SECTION ONE – setting massive goals for your revision.

Chapter 1 - What is it based upon?

This book is kind of in two sections. The first half is all about the setting of revision goals and personal goals. The second half is more of an action plan packed with fun and interesting ways of you being able to motivate yourself to learn and get better grades.

This section is dedicated to my long suffering friends and family who have put up with my annoying ways, short attention span, and joking around for way too long now. This book represents another MASSIVE goal ticked off my list of things to do before I step off the skateboard of life. Thanks "especially" to my wife Liz, my amazing son "George", my mastermind teams who kick my backside into gear and hold me accountable to get stuff done, and finally Neil Bakewell and Carl "the internet fox" Barton for pushing me through my fear of technology.

Before we go into the "how to use this goal setting process" let me give you some background on what this is based upon. Because if you're anything like me, perhaps you need some evidence as to where this information has come from, who else has used it and how will I know it will work for me?

Well, would you agree that sometimes you have to hear things in many different ways before the penny drops and you say: yes, I believe this information and I will use and apply it? It was exactly the same for me.

I was at school, an "average… AT BEST" student. I know that I could have achieved more but I was far too immature to focus, was VERY easily distracted, and really did not understand the significance of "why" I had to learn and gain knowledge and skills.

I was what people might call a grey student or C/D grade borderline student whose teachers at the time (or at least many of them) would say **"HYNER !!!!.... YOU can't do that"** and sadly…. I believed them because I left high school with C and D grades at best and with a fear and "at best" near-hatred of learning and education believing that I was not very bright.

Many years later working for myself as a chef running a small catering and event business I decided to ask some of my customers (who were the top achievers in the area) how they thought and behaved that made them so successful?

What they told me changed my life and I began to interview loads more successful top achievers as a hobby that then became more formal research.

I was about three years into my research (at the time of writing this I've been researching this for nearly eighteen years) and I managed to get an interview with, at the time, one of the richest men in the United Kingdom.

He was very, very successful as an entrepreneur and as a businessman. I was so excited. I was like a child in a sweetshop.

I couldn't contain myself I was so looking forward to interviewing this man and finding out how he thought and behaved when setting goals, because at the time he was the richest person I'd interviewed and I thought "he's bound to tell me the secret of success".

What I really wanted to know was how he set and achieved goals. And I asked him all the questions in the questionnaire up until the golden nugget question (as I called it). This question I was convinced would help me understand how top achievers think and behave, and how I could do the same. I asked him the question: "How do you think and behave? What is it you do differently to everybody else around you that makes you so successful? How do you set goals?"

And I was waiting pen poised, so excited, waiting for this fantastic answer that was about to come and he said,

"Well, I suppose all I do is, errrrm, **I set *big* goals**. Errrm, **think of things I might have to do** to achieve those goals. Errrm, **prioritise these things** and **take action**. Errrm, yeah, *I prioritise them, I take action* and I suppose **if I want it that badly, I never give in**. Hmmm, yeah, yeah, that's what I do." … And he said it in such a laid back way that I didn't believe he had taken the question seriously and I heard myself saying to him: "Excuse me, do you expect me to believe that your massive success is down to you - and I quote – 'setting big goals, thinking of things you've got to do to achieve those goals, prioritising those things, taking action and if you want it that badly, never giving in'?"

"Really?"

My friends, know when you've said the wrong thing! There was a silence. There was a pause you could have cut with a brick and then he almost spat down the phone at me: "Do you doubt me young man?"

At that point I was shocked back into reality and I realised that he was absolutely telling me the truth. After he said "do you doubt me" with such conviction I thought … wow, ok, I believe him. I finished the interview and I apologised for being so rude. In fact, after that incident I said "I'm sorry that must have sounded so rude". He said "It did! What's your point?" I said "I'm sorry, for me that was the most important question in the research and I didn't think you'd taken it seriously." There was a pause, and he said, "I can see why you think that, but do not doubt me. That is what I do." He left me in no uncertain terms, no doubt whatsoever that this is exactly what he did. It was exactly how he thought and behaved.

And you know when someone shouts at you, it kind of niggles you, you kind of carry it around in your head for the rest of the day. It eats away at you.

And well, he did that to me in a very positive way. And I went back to my office at home and I looked through all of the research papers that I'd done up until that point. I looked at the answers to that question and it just leapt out the papers at me. It was so obvious. Every single person that I'd interviewed up until that point and every single person since that time sets *big goals. Massive goals. Big fat hairy goals. Audacious goals. Huge goals. Dreams. Ambitions.* In eighteen years of interviewing the most successful people on the planet only one person when asked "how do you set goals" used the answer "realistic and achievable". This was a very successful businessman, an entrepreneur from America called Dr. Ivan Misner (a business networking guru). He answered the question "I set realistic and achievable goals David". I pointed out to him that any one of his massive achievements by anybody's benchmark would be huge and he said: "But David, I've achieved it. Therefore, it is both realistic and achievable."

And he made fun of it but then later admitted that when he set his goals he set MASSIVE goals.

What I am asking you to do is to set yourself some pretty MASSIVE goals to aim at.

"isn't that setting myself up for failure?" I hear you cry?

Be patient and you will learn why far from failure, that you by setting MASSIVE goals you actually are more likely to achieve your desired exam results and personal and academic goals.

The story of "Liz and the AS level she should never have got"

"I am working my socks off, and I understand the work, but when it comes to the exams I get so stressed that my brains freezes and I can not recall a thing !"

Liz was studying Chemistry AS level and after a few Months of going to college she was told that, with just three months to go before the exams, the college had been teaching the class the wrong syllabus. Once the anger had died down Liz took action. She got a coach/tutor on the subject who was first class at what they did (looked INTO), and decided that she was going to get her AS level Chemistry. I helped her learn how to use rhymes, songs and stories to remember things and she was seen revising to the tune of Disney songs and nursery rhymes.

She replaced the lyrics of the songs with the equations, formulae and processes that she needed to remember.

To the tune and the rythum of her favourite tunes, she remembered her Chemistry content.

In the exams, despite still being a little stressed she had such strong association to the music that she was able to recall nearly everything she had revised, and got an A* inside three months. Before this, as a student at High school she was told that she was not clever enough to go to University, and not to even attempt it. She went on to get a teaching degree, but also a dietetic degree, and a masters degree in autism studies. "Not clever enough…… REALLY ?!?!?!"

Still need convincing?

So my friends, answer this question if you can. If people at the very highest level, the people who achieve big, the super successful - if they set massive goals, why are we setting realistic and achievable goals?

Why are students in schools, colleges and universities being asked to set realistic and achievable goals?

Why are sales teams in organisations and major companies being taught to set realistic and achievable targets? My friends, 'realistic and achievable' sets people up to be nothing more than average at best. That quote came to me from the guy who founded Pertemps Recruitment - one of Europe's largest recruitment and employment companies … Mr Tim Watts.

When I said to him, "How do you set goals?" he fired back, as quick as a flash, "I set big fat hairy goals Dave." I said, "Sorry? What? Excuse me? You do what?" He said, "I set big fat hairy goals".

I said, "OK, are you aware that most people are being taught to set realistic and achievable goals?" And when he'd finished laughing, listen to what he said. He said, "David you're serious aren't you? You mean we're setting people up to be mediocre at best."

"realistic and achievable goals set people up for mediocrity … AT BEST !"

My friends, are the exam goals you set, setting you up to be mediocre … at best? Then let me ask you, is that acceptable? I think you're better than that. I think we're all better than that and it's only down to how we think and behave.

When I asked Jules Morgan how he set goals (Jules Morgan is world power boat racing champion and he's a world renowned marine design engineer) he quick as a flash, said, "I set huge goals Dave. Massive goals."

I said "Jules, are you aware that people are being taught to set realistic and achievable goals?" He said "David, can you name me anything of man or womankind's greatest ever achievements that would have been achieved if they'd have set realistic and achievable goals?" Can you think of anything? I couldn't and I still can't to this day.

Great things happen when – to begin with - one person believes it can be done.

Look throughout history at the things that have been achieved by man and womankind, the greatest achievements of the human race. It's normally happened when everybody believed it couldn't be done except for one person and then as soon as they did it, it was accepted as achievable. Somebody has to be number one. Somebody has to be top dog. Somebody has to be the leader in the field. Why not you? You can achieve big.

All you've got to do is set your goals big and then follow the process that we're going to teach you on this programme.

Have fun.

You know what? I've talked about Jules Morgan and the recruitment guy and the rich entrepreneur that I interviewed. Have you noticed something? They've all got these little quotes that they live their life by. Have you got a quote, a saying, something you live by?

Almost like a moral standard or a purpose statement. You might think it's a bit fluffy and woolly, a bit 'out there', but if they do it and they're achieving up there at the highest level, who's got it right?

Find something that you can live your life by. A little statement that will motivate you, inspire you, call you to action every time you think about it, every time you see it, read it or hear it.

Stick it on stickers around the house, put it on the sun visor in your family car so every time you pull it down, you see it. Stick it on your fridge, next to your desk, inside your purse or wallet, or handbag or school bag.

Put it on a sticker on the inside of your jacket so that every time you open it up, you see it, it inspires you and reminds you to take action and to be the person you need to be to achieve your goal.

Maybe if exams or revision stress you out your quote can be something like:

"I am calm, relaxed, and find my revision easy"

or…

"I cant wait to find out what I do not know or understand because that is where I will find the increase in my grades at exam time"

"I make my revision fun so that I am motivated to learn"

"when I get my awesome results I will treat myself by doing….."

"when my motivation is at its greatest, that is when I will study the subjects that scare me. Do the hard things first and the day then gets easier"

… or similar.

A group of tough young high school men were given three days with me and as part of the event I got top achievers to come in and speak to them. These lads were very challenging in their behaviour and their attitude stank on day one. They soon softened as they worked with Rock stars, sporting champions and successful business men. One of the top achievers was an Indian chap (and one of my dearest friends) called Satt Sembhy who started shifting gravel in a builders merchants yard when he left school and has now become one of the most successful luxury kitchen manufacturers and fitters in the UK.

The students were hanging on his every word and when it came to questions at the end, one young man shot his hand up and asked "what one thing would you say to all of us that we should do right now?"

Without hesitation Sat looked him square in the eye and from his heart said **"if you want to succeed and make yourself proud, you have no excuses… none at all ……. NO EXCUSES !!!"**

Many of their faces dropped a little as it dawned upon them that they were using various "excuses" not to be their best self. The quote "NO EXCUSES !!!" stuck with them.

What if you told yourself that you have "no excuses" and you gave your studies 100%?

So just before we get into the 'how' of setting goals allow me to just give you some background as to how I used this "MASSIVE GOAL" thinking to convince myself that this stuff really works, because when I started doing this I'd never achieved anything really significant myself. And I thought, well if top achievers do this it must work. But I've never achieved anything really big and so I thought what can I do that I've never done before? I thought to myself "I know I'll raise some money for charity. I've not done that before and it'll give me a chance to set a big goal and see if it works."

So I went into Birmingham to a little charity called The Crab Appeal.

C – R – A – B stands for Cancer Research At Birmingham. They were part of a bigger national cancer research campaign.

I stood before their fundraising committee that included inspiring men and women who were volunteers, but who were the Who's Who of Birmingham and the West Midlands. These were significant men and women, very well connected, very well thought of and they gave up their spare time to raise money and increase awareness for Cancer Research At Birmingham. I stood before them and I felt a very small fish in a very big pond.

I was embarrassed, I was terrified and I was fumbling my words and gripping a piece of paper with my notes on and shaking like a leaf before them. The chairman, God bless him, put his little round glasses on the end of his nose and looked over the top and said "So Mr Hyner, tell us what it is you want to do".

I looked at him and the other people around the table and I went "errrrm, errrrm I've interviewed some successful people.

They've told me how they set goals and I'd like to see if it works by applying it myself because they've told me they set big goals and I've never set big goals before, and I've never fundraised, I'm on my own, I've only got my spare time and I'd like to see if this stuff works by doing one event that raises you lots of money." And I thought they'd say "fantastic, tell us all about it".

But …… The chairman looked over his glasses at me and said, "With respect," And we all know what it means if people say it like that to you don't we? It means "with no respect whatsoever".

He said, "With respect, you're on your own, you've only got your spare time, you've never fundraised before and you want to raise... sorry, how much did you say?"

Now, I hadn't thought of a figure, and you know sometimes when you're put under pressure and you're asked to come up with some information and you just make something up?

And instead of thinking it, you hear yourself saying it and you say the wrong thing. Well, that was me. I said the wrong thing. I heard myself saying, "Fifty thousand pounds". As soon as I said it, the little voice in my head went "noooooooooo".

The chairman leant forward and said "Mr Hyner, there's seven of us, experienced fundraisers, well connected people. It took us six months of our spare time to organise our single biggest fundraising activity. It made a net profit of forty eight thousand pounds. You're on your own, you've only got your spare time and you're using a goal setting process that's not been proven. Thank you for showing an interest in cancer research. Goodbye."

Have you ever had anyone stick a pin in your dream balloon before? I was carrying my ego and my dreams in a sack on the floor behind me, dragging it out of the door. I felt so low. I felt like my legs had been taken from beneath me.

But then … have you ever had the opposite of that happen to you? Have you ever had a moment when one, just one, person believes in you?

They put their hand on your shoulder, and it's normally someone you'd least expect in my experience, and they say, "Come on … you can do this." That's all you need!

All of a sudden you become bullet proof. You become *fanfare*, "Yeah, I can do this!"

Well, one gentleman by the name of Melvin Evans, who at the time was treasurer of The CRAB Appeal, as he was showing me out the door with one hand, he put his other hand on my shoulder and leant over and said in my ear, "I think it'll happen, tell me more." I grabbed him. We went for a cup of tea together and over this short period of time we became very, very good friends.

But... did we raise £50'000 in one event I hear you cry?

Together, on our own, we ..... did **_not_** raise fifty thousand pounds.

No, we raised *over a quarter of a million pounds*. We smashed fundraising records for charities. We had an absolute ball of a time organising events that helped us achieve our personal lifetime ambitions and breaking charity fundraising records in the process. We proved the goal setting principle worked. Over the next six years I embarked on a personal crusade to prove this goal setting principle correct and, in my spare time, raised around five hundred thousand pounds for different charities, breaking numerous charity fundraising records along the way.

Here is a picture of our MASSIVE goal pyramid that we used to plan our goal, and I will show you HOW you can use a pyramid planner to achieve your goal later on.

My friends, once you use it for a personal goal and it works for you, you will use it in your academic life, you will use it in your school, college or your university. You can make it applicable to your sports team and your social life with your friends.

I dare you not to become more effective and more successful as a result of using our process. If you don't use it for a big goal I still dare you to use it just for your daily 'to do' list. We'll talk about that later on, but it will make you more effective and you will get so much more done.

The story of how "Maxsted MAXED out"

I regularly work at a private school in the UK and after one of my memory, goal setting and motivation skills workshops a student came up to me and said:

"Does this stuff really work mate?"

I told him "of course.. why do you ask?", and he went on to say how he had been doing okay in other subjects but in science he had been getting a D grade throughout school and that he really needed a C grade as a minimum because he wanted to study engineering at college.

I suggested to him that he had about four weeks between now and his mock exams at Christmas and if he followed our plan for just 5-10minutes a day, EVERY DAY for the next four weeks, that he could fully expect to be close to, or even achieve his C grade.

The young man left with a spring in his step, and after Christmas I returned to the school to deliver another workshop and as I walked across the car park the young man ran up to me and asked if I remembered him?

"Of course I do" I remarked, and asked "what grade did you get?"

"D" he exclaimed with a resigned sigh.

He admitted that he had not used the techniques as he believed that they would not work, but now he has nothing to lose and would use then for the next four months before his GCSE exam at Easter. I reminded him of the technique and off he went.

Maxsted was his name, and with some delight he contacted me after his results came through to tell me how he managed not to get a C grade but instead got a 100% A* grade !

BOOOM !!!!!

The story of "Danger Girl"

I had just finished presenting at a school in front of a group of two hundred 15 and 16-year-old students. As the students left the hall one young lady about 5 feet tall walked towards me with a menacing look on her face. As she approached she raised her arm and pointed at me and with a snarl she exclaimed, "It's all right for you!"

With hands out stretched I replied, "What do you mean it's alright for me?"

She marched straight up to me and said, "It is okay for you to say that we should set big goals and look into top achievers yeah? … but I can't achieve my goal!"

"What do you mean?" I replied.

"I can't achieve my goal!" she said.

"Why, what is your goal?" I asked.

She paused and said, "I want to be British junior downhill ski champion"

I'm ashamed to say that I nearly laughed out loud because not only did the young lady live in one of the flattest areas in the country, miles from any hills or mountains, but she was dressed entirely in black with metal piercings and tattoos, and my assumption was that this young lady would be one of the last people I would have expected to want to be a skiing champion. How wrong I was!

She said, "I am already third in the country but I will never be number one" and as she said this her face dropped, her tonality softened and her sadness was all too real to see. I could tell that she was telling the truth. A teacher standing behind her who could not see her facial expressions exclaimed, "No you are not… do not lie".

The student turned around to have a go at the teacher but before she could say a word, her friend jumped in and said, "Yes she is Miss but she doesn't tell anyone about it"

I asked, "Is that true… are you really number three in the UK?"

Without raising her head she nodded and said, "But you see mate, I am from a single parent family, no rich mom and dad to pay for coaching and competitions or travel".

"Who coaches you at the moment?" I asked.

"The local ski club captain" she said.

"What have they ever won?" I enquired.

"Local ski club captain" she smiled.

"RIGHT THEN!" I said….. "Off to the library for you, get onto a computer, get online and track down a world champion downhill skier and ask him or her to mentor you".

"They will not speak to me" she almost pleaded with a resigned tone. "You are making an assumption… go find out the truth" I said. By the time we had got back to our office we had been informed that the student had managed to get a coach, and a few weeks later we received an email from "DANGER GIRL" and the only words on the email were… "BRITISH JUNIOR NUMBER ONE !! … Thank you!"

Here is a pyramid goal planner used by an eleven year old school girl who started a business that made her "decent" money whilst she was still at school… !!!!

KEY POINTS FROM CHAPTER 1

1 -   Start thinking about a MASSIVE goal
for your grades

2 -   Look back at the times you have learnt
and achieved things and how you overcame

the challenges that faced you.

3 -   "NO EXCUSES !!!"

Chapter 2 - What is your goal?

… and what do you do if you have no goals?

So let's start by kicking off and telling you how to do this goal setting process. First of all….

- get online and find yourself an inspiring, motivational quote that you only have to read and it makes you want to jump up and take action on YOUR MASSIVE GOAL (the thing you have been putting off doing). Write the quote down on a piece of card and next to it or below it write a very specific and compelling goal for yourself.

"The more specific and the more compelling the goal is, the more likely it is to be achieved because your desire to achieve the goal is BIGGER than your fear of failure."

For example, if you want to be 'an athlete' you're less likely to become a successful athlete than if you were to tell yourself:

"I'm going to be world number one in the four hundred metres hurdles by 2030."

"I'm going to be world champion at ... by …"

Other goals might say…

"I'm going to have my own successful business doing ….."

"I'm going to get A stars in all of my exams."

"I'm going to win the award for best …. at..."

"I'm number one in my class (or school) at..."

Get specific. Nail down your goal. If you just have an airy fairy title to your goal your brain goes airy fairy on helping you to achieve it. If you have a specific goal your brain gets specific.

So what do you do if you haven't got any goals or if you don't know what it is you want to achieve in life or in school?

It is very rare in my experience that people "cannot be bothered… or do not care".

Most people who say they do not care are simply afraid of having a go for fear of looking silly if they fail, or are afraid of succeeding in case their friends no longer like them for standing out.

"Not bothered" is a lame excuse used by those who in most cases simply do not understand (as I didn't when at school) the consequences of their apathy and lack of action, or worse still, will fake a resigned sigh of disinterest to hide their lack of communication skills as they simply want to avoid challenging conversations of any type.

SMASH your objections with logic… "Not bothered" should now say "It's AVIN IT !"

The reason most people do not know what their goal is VERY RARELY because they do not have a goal….

But in nearly all cases, they have a few or many ideas and are afraid of taking action on any of them in case they pick the wrong goal to chase after. They fear failure, so do NOTHING! The fear freezes them into doing nothing and so they achieve……. Nothing.

Well let me ask you, are you happy?

Are you content with what you've got?

Are you happy with your lot?

If so, you're one of a rare breed, because most people say they are or say they're not and then whinge and moan about all the things they wish they could have done, should have done, would have done if....

…. I'd got more money

…. I'd got more time

…. I were more clever

…. I had more support

…. it was done for me

and many others.

Well you know what? If you keep saying things like that, you may as well just give up now because you'll get nothing done. What will happen if, one day, you retired, you're sitting in the nursing home looking out the bay window, with the tartan travelling rug over your legs, with a little bit of potato from lunchtime in the corner of your mouth. Would your head be full of memories or would it be full of regrets? Is it going to be full of, "Oh I wish I'd done that. I wish I'd had a go. I know I could have done it." Or is your head full of, " I did that" and your head is full of those memories, those senses, those smells, those sights, those sounds, those experiences, those emotions?

You decide.

Start by forcing yourself to say yes to as many opportunities that you can or want to do.

I once interviewed a top entrepreneur called Frank Bastow who lived by this mantra, and said that he had achieved in life by, **"Saying yes to opportunities and *then* working out how he was going to achieve them"**

Go and get those experiences right now. I want you to stretch your comfort zones. I want to you to go out and get new ways of thinking, new ways of behaving, go out and achieve some stuff. And I don't mean necessarily massive things. Maybe you just want to get better at a sport. Try a new hobby. Start a business, be it part time or full time. Maybe you want to travel?

Go!

There are ways of you being able to travel for nothing or even get paid to do it, if you look in to it. Maybe you can do things for charity right now. Don't wait. Go out and get those experiences. That way you can start being your ideal self before you become that person.

What do I mean by that? I mean for you to "be the person that you want to be". Don't wait to become that person. Start right now. If you want to be a recording musician, go into a studio and record a song. Don't wait until someone discovers you and pays you to do it.

Go and get that experience now and your self esteem will go through the roof. Your terms of reference based upon your experiences in life will go through the roof and your comfort zones expand. Go and get new ways of thinking, new ways of behaving.

Take action. If it's not working for you... Well, if what you're doing right now isn't working for you - change! What are the consequences to you of not changing, not thinking and behaving in new ways, not stretching those comfort zones? What are the consequences in five, ten, fifteen years time in your life?

What are the consequences to you of not achieving your goals to your work, to your business, to your career, to your qualifications to your family, your finances, your health?

My friends, take action.

Fourteen years ago I was terrified of speaking in public. The very thought of speaking in public filled me to my core with dread and fear.

I went out of my way to apply this stuff. I went to college and night school. I learned how to speak in public. I went out of my way to get experiences of speaking in public.

I studied top speakers and even got coached and mentored by a few of them. I joined a professional speaking association and learnt how to speak at their meetings. Fourteen years later, I'm now an award winning international professional speaker.

I speak in front of small groups, school groups, tens, hundreds, and even many thousands of people at events and major corporate audiences all over the world.

What is it that you can do that you want to do…. But are shying away from for nothing more than fear of the unknown?

Expand your experiences. Expand your comfort zone, and grow.

Go out and do the things *you* want to do, and *you* become the person *you* want to be.

You can use this goal setting process for daily 'to do' lists or a small goal, but I want you to now start thinking about a really large and very specific goal. Get an experience. Change your life.

It changes your thoughts and behaviours. By setting a really large and very specific goal you are already then thinking and behaving like a top achiever, and of course once you have done what ever it is that you are fearing, you have "done it" and so it can only be easier next time around.

Maybe you fear maths as a subject, or perhaps your level of reading ability is not your strong point and so you shy from dealing with it…. Or maybe you want to do exams early but are afraid to ask, or maybe you want to start a business whilst still at college but again do not know where to start, this will help you.

Set a day and a time when you can build your motivation and level of determination to take action on that thing until you are (even slightly) better at it. Set another day and time soon afterwards to go at it again, and so on until you have broken the back of your perceived "pain".

What are the assumptions that you're currently making about yourself and your abilities?

Are you saying positive or less helpful things to yourself, with that little voice in your head? (or is it just me that has little voices in my head? … lol… I do hope not).

Typically you've got a good voice and a bad voice.

You're good voice goes "Go on, have a go. You've always wanted to do it". You then might say "Go on then, I will" and you step outside your comfort zone.

You have a go at something and you go "Hey, this is good!". Later on you may trip up, you fail or you stumble or you drop your ball and you step straight back into your comfort zone because the bad voice kicks in and goes "I told you so… you loser, you are embarrassing yourself.

Don't stand out. Go back to doing what you've always done. Don't stand out." And sadly, which voice do we tend to believe the most and listen to the most,… the good voice or the bad voice? Nine times out of ten we listen to the bad voice. We tell ourselves we can't do it.

Well let me ask you, what is true? Ask yourself at the moments in your life where you've wanted to achieve something so badly, you've attached so much passion and excitement and conviction to it I bet nine times out of ten you've gone and actually done that thing.

Achieved it. So what's true? Nine times out of ten you can achieve or nine times out of ten you can't? Why do we believe that bad voice? Listen to the good voice my friend. Don't make assumptions about yourself and go and find out the facts.

Most of us can ride a bike yet none of us jumped onto the saddle first ride out and were able to cycle with ease and confidence.

There will have been a few falls, bumps and wobbles along the way, but we wanted to ride a bike so badly that we stuck at it.

So, how's it going for you? Really? I mean - the realistic and achievable goals we set, is that working for you? Are you super content, super happy with everything you've got in your life?

Yeah? … Brilliant!

No? … Well, try massive goals then.

The story of "Terrance"

A student messaged me on Facebook a few years after I'd done a presentation at his school. He suggested that he had used the MASSIVE goal principle to achieve his goal and his story inspired me.

Terrance said that he was a student that never stood out in any way. The school rarely paid any attention to him and by his own confession, he felt like he was drifting and life was happening to everyone else rather than to him. He had a dream of working in the merchant Navy however his attitude, and focus meant he was way off from achieving his goal. He left the presentation on MASSIVE goals and began to knuckle down, he looked at what he was doing at the moment, what he needed to be doing, and where he could improve. He went for it!

He said, "I used the massive goals pyramid to help me.

I isolated the areas that needed more attention and support to progress myself forward to where I wanted to get. As a result I am now a mercantile marine in the merchant navy. I didn't believe it was possible for me to change, but I did"

As a result Terrance got the grades he needed to got o college, and from there is now a mercantile marine in the British merchant navy where he operates a fleet support vessels in both the North sea and other areas providing emergency response, supply and underwater exploration / construction services to the offshore oil and gas exploration and production industry.

Terrance knew exactly what his goal was. He knew he had to change. He had the courage and maturity to look at himself, and his actions, and his situation, and identify what needed to change and what needed to be done to achieve his goal.

He then went after that goal ! ....

Terrance in charge of a support vessel.

Terrance onboard one of the Oil Rigs.

KEY POINTS FROM CHAPTER 2

1 - **Get specific in the wording of your goal**

2 - **SMASH your objections**

3 - **Say "YES !" to opportunities**

4 - **Go out and get experiences**

Chapter 3 - The 10% rule

Let's get more into the MASSIVE goal process. Let's help you to understand how you can set and achieve a massive goal now that we've given you some ways of thinking and behaving.

First of all, your goal must be **BIG.**

The bigger, the better.

If you want to raise ten thousand pounds for charity – go to raise twenty thousand pounds instead.

If you are getting C's and D's at school and you want B's and A's go for all A's.

If you want a company with a million pound turnover or profit go for two million pounds. Set the goal for double.

If you need to lose 5 Kilos in weight well, as long as it's healthy, go to lose ten instead.

If you want to learn how to read music set a goal to give and deliver a performance in front of people in public whilst reading music.

And, well, whatever it is just set it big. Allow yourself to get excited. Attach some passion to it. Make sure that your passion, that excitement, that reason for doing it is bigger than your fear and ... this is an important note, so sit up and take a note of this... Write it down.

Use big coloured pens. Circle it, stars round it, whatever you need to do. Find out your "*why*".

Have you got a purpose? Have you got a passion to achieve this goal? You've got to build that purpose and that passion to achieve the goal and make it bigger than your fear of failure. If you do that you should never, ever have any reason to give in. You will succeed in your goal.

If your purpose, your reason to achieve, if your level of excitement and passion is bigger than your fear of failure you will achieve your goal. You will succeed.

I know some people who founded a small but very effective charity. It's a British based charity working out in Africa. The charity is called Wyce. W – Y – C – E. It stands for Wonder Years Centre of Excellence. Instead of going out and building a well in a village in Africa, then going away and leaving them to it, they stayed in the village and they built a project helping the people of that African village to become better Africans - rather than trying to turn them into something they're not.

The charity work in the village developing healthcare, education and local skills and are so passionate about what they do.

When they speak to you their eyes sparkle. They have such a conviction in their voice, their tonality. They use gesture. Have you ever met anyone like that, who's got a real mission and a passion for things? You know what, if they failed would they give in or would they go back and have another go? Of course they'd go back and have another go! Why? Because their "why" is bigger than their fear of failure.

My friends … get that passion, get that purpose and never, ever give in. Get so excited that it makes you want to get out of bed early and run around taking action on your goal and achieving your goal.

If you know what you do, well, you're in the same bracket as everybody else.

You ask anybody who's got a goal and they will tell you what it is they do or what it is they want to do.

If you go to any business owner and say what is you do, they'll, or at least most of them would tell you in a heartbeat – bang – straight away, they'll give you an answer. If you ask them, *"Why do you do it?"* very few can answer with equal conviction and certainty. You ask people at the very highest level of anything, you ask top achievers, "Why do you do what you do?" and typically they can look you straight in the eye and give you a passionate, coherent answer. My friends, get a big enough "**why**". So now we've set a big goal.

The next thing is... think of things. Remember what that entrepreneur said ***"I set a really big goal, I then think of things that I've got to do to achieve that goal."***

 Find out what you don't know.

Now "that" scares most people. Do not get scared of what you do not know and what you do not understand, especially in relation to school work etc as it is only information and it "CAN" be learnt. We simply have to find a way of learning these new things that suit who "we are" as a person. How many students in schools and colleges do you know that won't put their hand up and ask for information to clarify their understanding for fear of looking stupid?

Get excited about what you do not know. In education, typically, at least in the UK, if you get an extra ten percent on your marks your grade goes up. By that I mean you go from a D to a C, or a C to a B, or a B to an A etc. An extra ten percent is usually enough to raise your game. If you find out what you do not know (or understand) and you go at it like a top achiever until you understand it, that is where you are going to get your ten percent from.

Typically when people revise for exams they simply go over the stuff they already know, just to feel good about themselves... and then, when their energy, motivation, time and resources are at their least, they then wonder why it's difficult to find out what they don't know. I will say it once again... *go after what you don't know whilst your energy, motivation, time and resources are at their greatest (at the start) because that's where you're going to get your ten percent from.* **Find out what you don't know and get excited by it.**

Could you imagine what an extra ten percent would do to your grades?

AN extra ten percent effort on revision?

An extra ten percent on making your own learning fun, engaging and motivating?

Could you imagine what an extra ten percent of effectiveness for your favourite sports team would do for them at the end of their season?

An extra ten percent in your health and well being?

An extra ten percent dedicated to your family, your partner, your loved ones?

An extra ten percent in your savings?

Find out what you don't know, get your ten percent, ... it changes your life.

The story of Joseph

I'm in an inner city school on an estate called Castle Vale on the edge of Birmingham, England. Students slowly leave the hall after my goal setting and memory skills workshop and towards me walk a small group of young men pushing one of their group.

I at once assume that they are picking on him and if there is one thing I cannot abide, it is a bully, so I jump off the stage area and walk up to them asking what the problem is. They do not even look at me but instead push their chosen victim towards me saying, "Go on... show him!"

"Show me what?" I enquired, as I stood between the group and the now embarrassed boy.

The "alpha" male in the group looked at me and said, "He is an amazing artist sir and he could do really well but he didn't want to show you his work"

I had read the situation wrong. They were not picking on him. They were trying to help him but sadly his shyness and attitude were preventing him from asking for help.

"Show him the ******* pictures Jo!" they insisted yet again.

"Go on mate" I said, "I would love to see them"

He tried one last time to walk away but they grabbed him and pushed him back. They were determined not to let him get away. He slowly opened a portfolio he was carrying that showed the most incredible design drawings of what looked like futuristic car interiors.

"You did these…?" I asked open mouthed in amazement.

"Yeah… but its just a dream… I wanted to be a graphic designer for the motor industry but what chance have I got when I live on the Vale?" and with that he bowed his head. His friends slowly drifted away almost knowing that they had done all they could do and the rest was up to Joseph.

*I challenged him on how serious he was about his dream and he convinced me of his desire to achieve. Was he willing to **give an extra 10%** effort to kick start his goal into action. With his parents and the schools permission we hooked him up with Jules Morgan, a renowned design engineer who kindly offered Joseph work experience followed by an apprenticeship based on his ability and work ethic displayed during work experience. What Joseph learnt during his time with Jules was :WHY" he needed maths, physics and English, and he went back to school and improved his attitude, performance….. and results! .*

10% can go a long… long way to your success.

KEY POINTS FROM CHAPTER 3

1 -   Know your "why" or purpose

2 -   Find out what you do not know …

        and get excited by it

3 -   Work on your 10%

Chapter 4 - The art of looking "INTO"

This next thing is crucial. Write this down. Big red ink, stars around it again, fluffy clouds, whatever floats your boat. I want you to make a big note of this:

 Find somebody to look into.

One of British athletics heroes is the 400m runner Kriss Akabusi. Kriss, is a successful, energetic and most generous man who has succeeded in many areas of life. When I asked Kriss for the one thing that had helped him succeed the most, he replied, **"Top achievers should be looked into, NOT up to!"**

With his permission I share his message with thousands of students every year and it has helped so many people to achieve quite amazing results.

#ThanksKriss #legend

You know what, too many people look up to successful people. Many people go "Oh, aren't they great, aren't they this, aren't they that". They place these successful people in their mind on some kind of pedestal considering them to be superior to themselves in some way. Don't look up to people (said Kriss). Nobody is better than you. You are as good and as worthy as anybody else. Do not let anybody determine what it is that you are capable of achieving. If somebody's really, really good at something that you want to be good at, if someone's great at business, if someone's great at studying mathematics, if someone's great at sport, if someone's great at relationships and you want to be better at any of that stuff find someone who's amazing at it and don't look up to them – *look into them*. Find out how they think and how they behave when they're doing what it is that they do. If you go to average people or reference sources to get your information, you're going to get average information …. AT BEST! If you go to a top achiever for your information, what kind of information are you going to get? Of course, the best information! So my challenge to you is find someone to look in to. I dare you to approach top achievers for help, support, coaching and mentoring.

Sorry top achievers out there in the world … you're going to get inundated now with these supercharged goal setting people wanting to achieve at the highest level and wanting to understand how you think and behave (I hope). I consider it your place in society to serve them as best as you are able.

I dare you. Find someone to look into. Do whatever it takes though (legally and ethically) until they let you stand in front of them or interview them over the telephone so that you can get inside their heads and understand how they think and how they behave. And all you have to do then is do the same as they suggest.

If you want to be a world champion, you've got to think and behave like a world champion now. To quote Mahatma Ghandi, you've got to, **"be the change you want to see in the world"**. If you want to be a world champion, you've got to think and behave like a world champion now. Then and only then can you become a world champion.

The story of the shy student and the American president

A tall, slim young lady sidles up to me after an event and suggests that she does not know where to start when it comes to her MASSIVE goal as nobody takes her seriously. Upon asking a few questions to determine what her goal is she suggests she wants to go into International politics. I of course suggest that she should do what Kriss Akabusi suggests and get a mentor who is in politics but make sure that they are playing at the highest level.

"WHAT !?… ME !?... speak to a politician?" she asked with a face of fear.

"YES!" I replied

"Oh… okay…" she mumbled and walked away.

Now I have been known to have that effect on women but not quite that bad… lol.

I thought nothing more of it until a few weeks later when I received a telephone call from the then head of sixth form at the school asking;

"Do you encourage young women to harass the president of the United States of America?"

"Errrrrr…….. maybe..?" I replied… "Have I done something wrong?"

"No" he laughed, "I am winding you up David, but I have been speaking to the head of security at the White House in Washington and they have informed me that it is quite rare for a student to get a written reply from the president"

My jaw dropped as it dawned on me what this young lady had achieved. It transpired that she had (with her parents and the schools support) written to Barack Obama and had received a written reply answering her questions.

I bet her CV had "coached by the president" on it somewhere … lol

Name the one subject or topic within a subject that you really struggle with?

Now name me one subject or topic that (for whatever reason) you excel at and find easy?

Offer your services to people who struggle with the thing you are great at, but who are great at the thing you struggle with? A revision buddy and accountability partner. Push each other on your respective areas of weakness until you have gained your 10%... or more.

For example, if I had known this at school I would have found somebody good at maths (my weakness) who needed help with creative writing (my strength).

KEY POINTS FROM CHAPTER 4

1 - **Get (look into) a mentor at the highest level**

2 - **"Be the change" … that you need to be doing**

Chapter 5 - Brainstorming

Next we go into a brainstorming process. You've got to go crazy with this one. Get some friends round, people who have different skills and talents to yourself. If you are a very studious, a dot your **i**, and cross your **t** type person, an "everything must be just perfect" kind of person, surround yourself with live wires, some creatively minded people.

If you're a creatively minded person surround yourself with people who are studious and good at fine detail.

People who will stop you in your tracks and hold you to account to make sure you get the fine detail done.

Find out what you don't know.

Write down the big things you've got to do to achieve your goal, the little things you've got to do to achieve your goals.

Write them all down in a big list. Brainstorm everything you can think of, you've got to do in order to achieve your big goal.

Then, before you prioritise these things…..

I want you to consider starting a Mastermind group.

Mastermind groups were something that started at the age of the industrial revolution. Leading industrialists, socialites, scientists, philanthropists, philosophers, entrepreneurs and captains of industry would travel to places in and around the West Midlands in the UK. I believe later on these groups also sprung up in other parts of the UK and in other industrial nations like America. Lunar societies and Lunar groups (mastermind groups) were meeting that used to meet for a couple of days.

They used to share each other's opportunities and challenges.

They used to brainstorm solutions to these challenges and then between meetings they would support each other and hold each other accountable on the tasks they set themselves to achieve between meetings.

Typically, they would have a process to their meetings.

They would begin by feeding back on what they've done since last meeting, what they've achieved and what they haven't done.

Then they would brainstorm each other's opportunities or challenges.

Then they would commit to doing things between now and next meeting and then they would support each other and hold each other accountable between the meetings to keep each other on track.

The reason most of us do not achieve our MASSIVE goals is because we do not get the right support and we do not allow others to hold us truly accountable.

I facilitate some Mastermind groups and just to give you two very quick examples of two people who really stuck at the process diligently.

- One gentleman who already thought he had a really profitable business, very successful, couldn't possibly achieve any more - in one year nearly doubled his turnover, increased his profits astronomically and had twice as many holidays than he's ever had before.

- Another gentleman, in a two year period, got out of a substantial amount of debt and some great personal challenges to set up a business that's now on target to make him a substantially wealthy man and he's the happiest he's been in years.

Set up a Mastermind group. Get people around you with different personality styles that will support you and hold you accountable.

Because, if you surround yourself with people who are just like you it will turn into a fireside chat and you'll get nothing done.

KEY POINTS FROM CHAPTER 5

1 -   **Brainstorm your challenges and things**

        you do not understand to get ideas on

        how you might approach things

        differently.

2 -   **Set up a mini mastermind group**

Chapter 6 - Prioritising your "to-do" tasks

So...

√ we've set a big goal

√ We've thought of things we've got to do to achieve the goal.

√ We're looking into people.

√ We've got a Mastermind group.

√ We've got our motivational quotes.

This is great stuff...... well done !

Now, we prioritise. Look at the list of all the things you've got to do that came up with during the brainstorming process. The big things, the small things, the stuff you've brainstormed, all the ideas that will, we hope, enable you to achieve your goal.

Now we place them in an order of importance.... Importance for you in terms of what you perceive as the most important things that have got to happen first if you're going to achieve your goal.

Prioritise your list into the most important things, the next most important things and then the least important tasks.

Maybe number them, with number one being the most important and so on. If you ever have had a lot to get done in a day, do you do yourself a 'to do' list? If you just look at this as a list would you agree that many of us have a tendency (through laziness or fear) to do the easy stuff first so that we can cross the task off the list and feel good about ourselves, and then the big stuff never gets done?

Well, you know what …?

We're going to draw a pyramid. We're going to draw a huge, dirty great big triangle. And, for example, if you've got twenty things on your brainstormed list of things to do, I want you to draw a pyramid with forty blocks in.

If you've got a hundred things on your list of things to do, draw a pyramid with two hundred blocks in.

That is so that you do not have to rewrite a plan if other ideas crop up (that you have not yet thought of in your brainstorming process), you just populate an empty box in your pyramid.

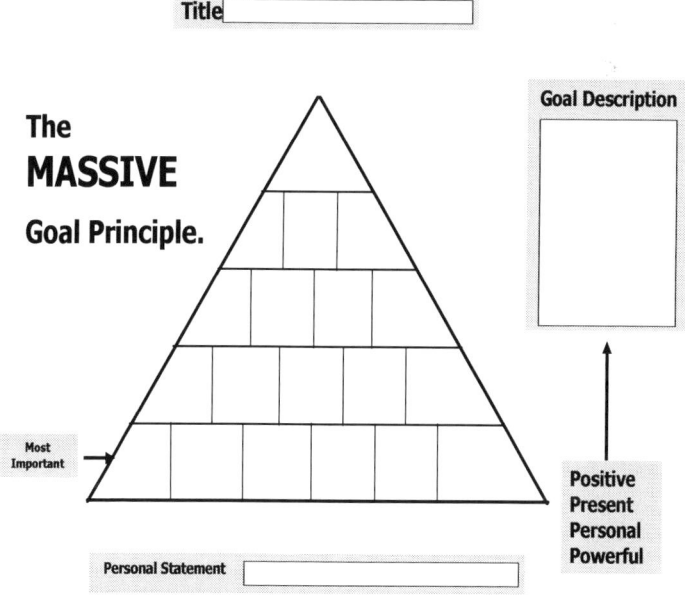

TITLE; give your goal a powerful title that inspires you !

GOAL DESCRIPTION; in a sentence describe what you will be achieving.

Write this in a positive, present, personal and powerful tense.

Not... "I want to run my own business" but more like;

"I run my own successful online shop that makes a real difference to others"

PERSONAL STATEMENT; write an inspiring quote that will keep you motivated.

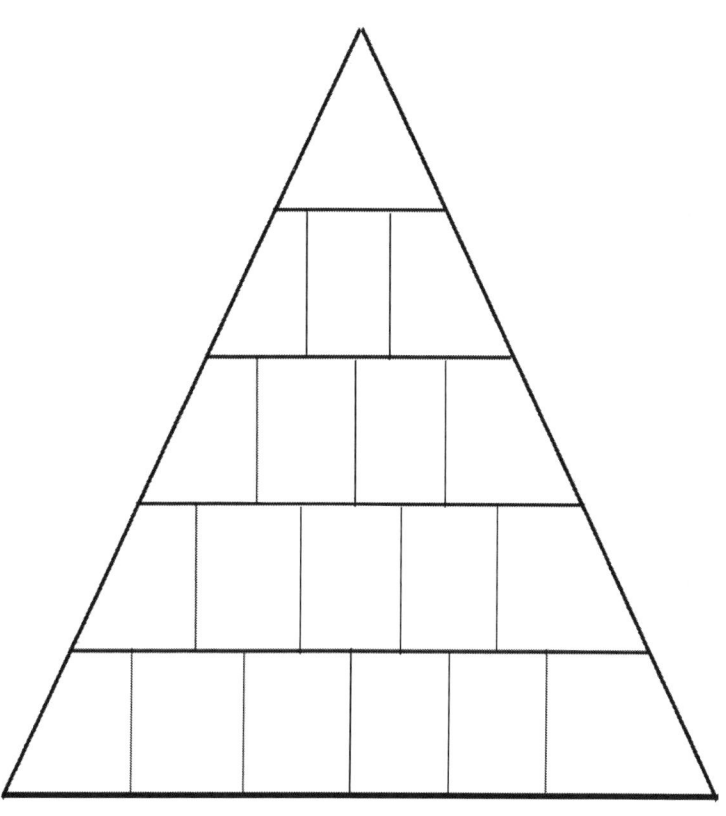

Above is a blank pyramid for you to use as a trial for your daily to-do list.

If you prefer to use technology there is a superb piece of goal setting software (part of which has a pyramid planning option as it was designed by a goal setting client that loved our work) available at https://www.goalstormer.com/login.php?regitemtyp e=referral&referredby=56

There is also an online video course on this subject available at

https://www.udemy.com/the-massive-goal-principle/

Allow me to explain.

So, draw a pyramid. Draw a big triangle and draw lots and lots of rows into your triangle and in each row along the bottom put in blocks. So if, for example, you've got about forty or fifty things in your pyramid you might draw a dirty great big triangle and in your bottom row, along the bottom of the pyramid, the base of the pyramid, you might have ten or eleven or twelve boxes in that row.

The row above it you might have ten or eleven boxes.

The row above that eight or nine boxes.

The row above that six or seven boxes.

And so on and so on until you go up your pyramid filling each row with blocks and you've got double the amount of blocks than you have items on your list to do.

This is the easy bit. Now maybe you will have yourself one HUGE pyramid with all of your subjects in, having prioritised them all so that you work on the hardest things first, or maybe you will do yourself a smaller pyramid for each subject?

If there is a topic that terrifies you BIG TIME, I would suggest that you did a pyramid just for that one topic (it would have been algebra for me) until you look at every box or task and know that on its own, that you can nail it.

Put the most important task in the bottom left hand block on the bottom row, and you sequentially fill in the boxes of your pyramid from left to right along the bottom row, left to right along the next row, with the most important tasks in the bottom blocks and rows of your pyramid.

Use only one or two words at most in each block to describe the task so that it is easy to read.

Maybe even think of an image that best represents the task, and remember that it only has to make sense to you because it is … your goal.

Hopefully you've half filled your pyramid or a third filled your pyramid with tasks to do. If something else crops up, all you do is populate an empty box. You've got foundations in place because a pyramid, just like any building, under the ground has foundations and without those foundations the building would eventually collapse.

The same principle applies with MASSIVE goal setting, if you haven't got foundation tasks (MUST DO TASKS) your goal will not be achieved because you will be inclined to spend all your time whilst your motivated doing the easy stuff, the feel good stuff and then the big things will not get done.

My friends, set a big goal, think of things you've got to do, prioritise them and take action on the big things first. Here's another thing to highlight, asterisk, circle, put a cloud around, stars around: *Link your personal goals and motivations or rewards to your revision goals.* For example, I used to love trekking in remote locations. I loved walking. One year, instead of doing it for charity, I organised a group of business people to trek in Peru and they ended up, basically, paying for me to go trekking in Peru. I did it for no fee. No fee to me whatsoever. How could you achieve your lifetime goals and it not cost you a penny?

Maybe you could do it for charity. Maybe you could do all sorts of things if you really put your mind to it. Build in incentives and rewards for yourself. Perhaps at the end of each row put in a little reward for yourself for having achieved so much.

In relation to revision, how about planning to reward yourself with social time, sport time, computer or gaming time etc, once you have mastered one of the things that you were struggling with?

Eg; Once I have nailed algebra I will allow myself an hour on the console, or chatting with friends etc.

But remember, you must build your goal on solid foundations. If you take action on the big stuff first, the goal gets easier and easier. I dare you. Prioritise those tasks into a pyramid and take action.

KEY POINTS FROM CHAPTER 6

1 -   Prioritise your tasks or to-do list

2 -   Plan your pyramid/s

Chapter 7 - Taking Action

So....

- √ You have set a big goal.
- √ You have thought of all the things that you have got to do in order for you to achieve your goal.
- √ You have prioritised these tasks and you've populated your pyramid.

Hopefully your pyramid is half or a third full of things and you're looking at the bottom rows and blocks and you are looking at it and going, "Yep, those are the most important things." Further up you are looking at the tasks there in the next rows and blocks and going, "OK, yes, those are the maybe 'to do' things if there's time and if they are needed." Ok, yeah, and you are looking at the blocks further towards the top and you go "Ok, those are the incidentals, the things that will get done over time if needed, the easy stuff".

What I want you to do now is…

"take action" on that bottom left block. The most important thing that you've identified will catapult you closest and quickest towards achieving your goal. That thing might be big, it may be scary, it may even seem huge…. But whilst your motivation is at its greatest go "rhino" on it !!!

Put *all of your energy* into achieving that task. Because, would you agree, that if you have done this properly by,

- √ Choosing a MASSIVE goal with a big enough purpose
- √ having a mentor to look into and/or a mastermind group
- √ brainstorming
- √ prioritising

… you can look at the list, look at the blocks in your pyramid and would you agree that each task on its own is both realistic and achievable?

If the only thing you had to do was that bottom left block, could you do it? Yes or no?

If the only thing you had to do was the next block? Could you do that? Yes or no?

My friends, if you can answer "yes" to every single block the only thing that's stopping you is willpower and a bit of hard work. If by chance there is still one or two blocks that on their own you think are "too big", if you think "ooh, that's still a bit frightening. I don't know it, I don't understand it" … all you have to do is take that block and do a pyramid and brainstorm that block into a separate pyramid. So you might have a master pyramid for the major goal and maybe one, maybe a handful at most, of little sub-pyramids on different pieces of paper that will help you break down every single big task until you look at them all and say;

"I can do that. I can do that. **I – can – do – that**."

If you set a goal like that everything gets easier. The more you do, the more you take action on the big chunky ones the little chunky ones just seem to happen. It builds its own unstoppable momentum. Set a massive goal, but have realistic and achievable blocks in your pyramid.

So, is each block a realistic and achievable task? If so my friends, take action. If not, do a pyramid with smaller blocks until you look at everything you've got in front of you and you say to yourself **"I – can – do – that".** Act on the most important tasks.

Get your diary, get your diary and a pen right now … and diary time, allocate time, set time aside to do these tasks.

If you've got a lunch break, if you say "I can't, I'm at school or I work full time."

No! Take a break.

Go to the toilet. Get on the mobile phone, make a call that will take you one step closer to achieving your goal. Instead of going out for lunch or sitting with your mates listening to music moaning and whingeing, go outside, go for a walk, get on the phone. Take some action. Write a letter, get a laptop, borrow a laptop or a PC. Write a letter. Send an email.

Get somebody to look into.

Get yourself a mastermind group.

But, take action.

Here is a pyramid goal planner I used to organise a trek in Peru in 2007.

The story of the rapper

When I was at school there was an inspiring teacher called (hope I spell his name right?) Bob Spalek. He was an Ox of a man who had represented Great Britain at power-lifting which tells you of his size. He was a firm but fair man, and stood for no nonsense in his classroom.

Many years later as an adult embarking upon my speaking career, I was amazed when I did my first ever talk in a school, to find that the headmaster was the one and only Bob Spalek.

After my talk he invited me into his office and asked if I would help one student that was about to get kicked out of school, but who had real potential. The student wanted to study medicine at university (something that very few from that school has achieved in history) but his behaviour and attitude was so bad, that he was more likely to get expelled from school, than sit his exams.

After a very tense and heated exchange I discovered that the issue lay at home where the family situation was so tense that he was unable to fit in and seemingly, everything he did was wrong. So, he displayed his unhappiness at school where he knew he would face less of a consequence for his actions.

After another heated exchange I discovered that his passion was for rap music and hip-hop. I challenged him to rap his revision, and he accepted the challenge.

I was told by the school that he flew through his exams, and ended up doing well at university and was now doctor serving his community and doing very well.

Could you "rap" your revision?

Could you reggae your revision?

… rock?

… RnB?

…. The answer is yes.

To the tune and the beat of your favourite songs, fit your revision replacing the lyrics.

So instead of "twinkle twinkle little star" (as the nursery rhyme goes), you might to that tune and rythum fit an equation, formula, date, statistic or piece of text etc that you needed to recall.

Make your own learning fun !

KEY POINTS FROM CHAPTER 7

1 -   Break down every task into "realistic and achievable" steps

2 -   Look at each task and make sure you "CAN DO IT"

3 -   TAKE ACTION … on the hardest bottom blocks first !

Chapter 8 - Never give in!

So, you've set a big goal, you've thought of the things that you've got to do to achieve the goal, you've prioritised them into a pyramid and now you're taking action.

The last thing is something you might think is just a semantic, but all the top achievers I've interviewed allude to this and that is: *If you've got a big enough "why" or purpose, you don't bail out and give in anywhere near as easily. You just found a way of it not working yet.* By that I mean, if you were to interview any scientist, any inventor and you were to say to them "Well, I tried that and I failed so I gave up" they would look at you with a blank expression as if to say "Why?" Scientists and inventors never give in. If they have a big enough reason to achieve what it is they want to achieve.

Now, what is it you're going to do? Have you got a big enough "why"? Nine times out of ten if you really want something, if you've got a big enough reason to achieve it … do you fly or do you fall? Nine times out of ten do you listen to the positive voice, the one that says "go on, have a go. I dare you." Or, do you listen to the negative voice? The one that says "Can't. I'm not good enough. I don't understand it. I need to fit in with my friends. I am not liked by others. I'm broke." My friend, don't make assumptions. You are more capable than you dare imagine. If you want to convince yourself that you are amazing, if you want to convince yourself that you have capabilities beyond your wildest dreams I dare you to go and look into and maybe interview one of the paralympic sports champions of our time. Go and track these people down, people with seemingly huge challenges and every excuse under the sun to "not achieve" .. who have gone on and achieved at the very highest level. They will make you feel very, very humble and just a little ashamed that if they can do this stuff what have I got to whinge and moan about?

My friends, take action. Don't make assumptions about your capabilities. Discover what is true. Go and get experiences in life. Stretch yourself. Jump, leap, positively propel yourself out of your comfort zone. Because who decides what you're capable of achieving? Know your "why". Is it bigger than you fear?

On that subject, who decides what it is that you are capable of?

We can all at times be guilty of blaming other people or situations for controlling our abilities to achieve when in most (not all) cases, the outcome is in our own hands.

Lynns story

There's an inspiring woman that I met many years ago. Her name is Lynn Grocott. When I first met Lynn she was emotionally and physically quite challenged. She was ill, very ill. She has multiple sclerosis. She walked bent over almost double at times when it was at its worst. Every step was agony for her. She had those big walking sticks in each hand, the ones with the support that goes up the forearm.

Every step was agony and she literally "ouched, oohhhd, ahhhd" her way with the smallest of fairy steps down the corridor of the hotel when I first met her on a training event that I was speaking at.

Just by allowing herself to believe two words, she changed her life.

In recent years Lynn has gone from being someone who in her life has been on the wrong end of physical and sexual abuse, and had to experience the suicide of both of her parents. She came through a drug addiction, an eating disorder and the loss of her great and quite inspiring husband to cancer.

Despite all of this Lynn, with her multiple sclerosis, has decided that she decides what she is capable of. Every day she says to herself "I decide what I'm capable of achieving. Life is not a dress rehearsal so give it your best shot"

Nobody else decides what she's capable of achieving. Lynn has become a successful author, she has her health more managed in a way that enables her to do lengthy cycle rides to keep herself supple.

Sure she still has a few challenges with her MS, but now she swims to raise money for charity.

*She walks "more normally" than she once did. She is a proficient schools speaker. She marches up and down the stage like a caged tiger ramming home a message of **"you decide"** to students all over the country.*

And, well, in her spare time she raises money for charity. She's raised enough money that enabled the building of a mother and baby until out in Africa. She's a successful coach and gives her time to help support those who need emotional support.

This woman is, quite frankly, amazing. And all she says is "nobody determines what I'm capable of achieving. I decide."

What if you took those two words as your mantra, your message, your motivational quote for yourself? You decide. Never, ever give in. You decide.

Remember Satt Sembhys quote … "NO EXCUSES !"

Sure, tough decisions will need to be made, and that reminds me of the tennis champion that I interviewed called Mark Eccleston. A crazy guy and really great fun to be around. Quite inspiring to hear of what he's achieved. I haven't got the space to tell you all his achievements, I would be here all day. But he had just signed professional terms with a rugby league club when he was being silly with some friends and he had a terrible accident that left him paralysed in his lower torso and legs. He has an amazing attitude to life and went on to represent Great Britain in various sports including wheelchair rugby and tennis and also became Britains first world number one tennis champion. He said one thing that was so profound to me.

He said "David, I was asked by a student in a school, what is the definition of success?" He said "I thought that was such a great question Dave and I answered it like this:

"There were days when it was cold, it was throwing it down with rain and I had to make a decision. I could either go to the bar with my friends or I could go training. I chose training. I became world number one."

The question is, what are you doing? What decisions are you making? Are you choosing to veg out in front of the TV every night, when you could be making a better decision? I will do an extra ten percent revision. I will do an extra ten percent ont hat topic I am struggling with. What decisions are you making? Success is not about what you achieve to these people. Top achievers will tell you this. **Successes to them are the micro decisions**, every single day, that you make. Be the change you want to be. You decide.

If you want something that badly, you go after it, otherwise wherever you go, there you are.

What do I mean by that? Wherever you go, there you are. I believe it's almost like a Buddhist philosophy.

Wherever you go, there you are.

What that means is if you go after something to make you happy, you might or might not achieve it, but you'll still be the same person whether or not you've achieved it. The top achievers get happy and then go after things. They become the change or the person that they want to be.

Mahatma Ghandi's quote again "be the change you want to see in the world".

If you want to be a world champion, you've got to think and behave like a world champion to become a world champion. So think and behave like a world champion my friends. Be the change that you want to see in your world. Never, ever give in.

And so, to conclude, here are the key points of this short book that if used could change your life forever.

> You've set a big goal.
> You've thought of things that you've got to do to achieve the goal.
> You've prioritised those things into a pyramid.
> You're taking action.
> You're never going to give in.
> You have a big enough purpose to overcome your set backs and fear.
> You have a coach or mentor or mastermind group at the highest level.

I'm going to leave you in the first section of this book with this last message.

"You decide. Do not let anybody or anything ever determine what it is that you are capable of achieving."

Tims story

I facilitated a mastermind group full of business men who were doing quite well, but all of whom wanted to do "very" well.

At the third meeting we were discussing purpose as a concept and how our core values and our insecurities determine who we are and therefore our purpose in life. A quiet, logical and unassuming member of the group called Tim who was not known for saying too much piped up with "I have no insecurities!"

The whole group turned and looked at him, then looked to me to see how I was going to deal with this.

"Tim" I said… "surely everybody has at least a couple of insecurities do they not?"

He lowered his head and began to doodle with his pen. Most unlike Tim.

"I used to have too many insecurities to mention until I was told that I only had a few months to live"

Nobody knew if he was serious or not and so we asked if he was serious and it turned out that Tim had been a very successful accountant, finance director and consultant and had, for all his life, hidden his fears and insecurities behind his success putting on a front of confidence that belied his weakness inside.

"I had too many to mention" he said "but when you are told that you have a finite amount of time left to live you very quickly realise that all… and I do mean EVERY SINGLE ONE of the things that you were ever afraid of, or held as a weakness or insecurity, mean nothing at all and they hold no fear for you because in THAT moment you know them to be of no significance"

He went on to talk about how money, cars, houses, investments and reputation at work mean very little in practical terms. He knew in that moment that what really mattered were the things that he thought he had not given enough time to such as his wife, his children… and himself.

"If I could have my time again I would focus on what really matters" he said.

*It is for this reason that I close with Tim's story because the most vital part of goal setting and "any" achievement is to first ensure that you know **why** you are doing what want to do and focus on the right things.*

I have worked with too many chief executives who have worked their whole lives, doing silly hours at work believing that they were doing it for their family, only when challenged to ask their families what "they" wanted, to be told that they wanted more of them at home.

Know *why* you do what you do !

From now on do not make negative assumptions about what you are capable of achieving. Use the Massive Goals Principle and from now on…

YOU DECIDE !

KEY POINTS FROM CHAPTER 8

1 -   Go and train in the rain

2 -   NEVER give in

3 -   YOU DECIDE !

4 -   Success lies in your smallest of

decisions and choices

If you prefer to use technology there is a superb piece of goal setting software (part of which has a pyramid planning option as it was designed by a goal setting client that loved our work) available at https://www.goalstormer.com/login.php?regitemtype=referral&referredby=56

There is also an online video course on this subject available at

https://www.udemy.com/the-massive-goal-principle/

Section Two

SECTION TWO – key revision tips, techniques and things to do.

In the second section of this book we share some fun and interesting ways of you being able to motivate yourself to learn and get better grades. There really is something for everyone.

This section is dedicated to the amazing top achievers I have interviewed over the years who inspired me to believe in myself and take action the way I hope this book is doing for you. It is a shout out to those who believed in me when others doubted.

Those "cool" teachers, role models and mentors in my youth who have shaped me (Mr Cattell, Mr Lomax, Brian Sheldon, Les Cusworth, Kevin Moran, Mrs Aldritt, Mr Dyson, John Cooper and others) along the way.

In my career as a schools trainer and speaker I have met and been inspired by great teachers (way too many to mention here but you "rhinos" know who you are).

However the real glory goes to the students over the years who have taken action with the information contained within these pages and have amazed themselves, their families and their teachers with results that far surpassed their wildest expectations.

I know and believe that you can do the same.

Chapter 9 – EXCUSE BUSTING !

So, you've set yourself a goal, you have got yourself all excited saying things like "this time I mean it, I am really going to revise hard", set your desk and books up, and planned where you will get your ten percent from, but then what?

You will use any excuse to get out of revising yeah?

Chatting with your mates

TV looks good

Try and beat your best score on the latest game

Spend time with your girlfriend/boyfriend

Listen to music

Sleeping

Can't understand it anyway so what's the point?

Can't be bothered

… the list can be endless when it comes to creative ways to avoid doing what we need to do eh?

I want you to write down your three biggest excuses that you use or have that have prevented you from revising in the past. Be brutally honest with yourself.

1)

2)

3)

Now I want you to pretend that you were coaching your best friend who was struggling and you needed, and wanted to help them.

They tell you their three excuses (same as yours written above) and I want you to list at least five ideas or pointed questions that would or could possibly help them to take positive action towards their revision goals.

For example, if a friend gave me an excuse that "I am not interested in revision", I would suggest things that might include the following possible list of things (minimum of five ideas).

a) Help them to understand and (if still not interested) accept the consequences of not revising and not getting decent exam grades to their finances, job prospects, self esteem, employability, friendship groups as they move onto bigger things etc.

b) How could they use something that they are interested in (such as music) to help you revise?

c) Could they use a reward or consequence to motivate them? For example, if they get decent grades they could go on holiday or if not they would have to sing in the high street dressed as a smurf..... okay maybe not a smurf but you get the idea eh?

d) Could they work with a few friends who also have given up or been given up on to work together to show people that they can achieve and prove a few people wrong?

e) Ask them what they want to be or achieve in life and then compare those doing that job to the reality of not revising.

Pick the most motivating one of your options and take immediate action on it. I mean NOW.... Go and do something positive towards the goal NOW !!!!!!

It is the procrastination (putting off doing stuff) that paralyses us, and when we are most afraid we use rubbish excuses like the above to pretend we are not bothered when we really do care but are afraid of saying so.

The fear and stress paralyses us and we hide behind the mask of … "whatever".

I see it all the time when working with teenagers who put their "too cool for school" face on and mutter "whatever" under their breath when all the time they are seeking help and support to show them "how" to do something that they are "pretending" not to care about.

"BUST" your excuses before you start revising and motivate yourself to learn. Do not wait to be inspired. Go and find an inspiration of your own. **OWN IT !!!**

KEY POINTS FROM CHAPTER 9

1 -   List all of your excuses to "not" revise

2 -   Think of reasons to BUST that excuse

3 -   BUST THAT EXCUSE !

Chapter 10 – Have A Timetable.... And Start EARLY!

This is going to be a short chapter because there is little more to do that having yourself a plan and sticking to it. If you were to do this, it must only work.

If your style is to sit for hours with your head in a book, and that works for you, then I suggest you do just that. For myself, and I know, countless others of you for whom that is NEVER going to be a plan, I suggest that you break the day down into periods of each day allowing for revision time, planning time, free time, and any other jobs or duties you have to fit in around your learning. **Maybe colour code them?**

For example:

ERT   = Easy Revision Time (subjects that are easy to do)

HRT = Hard Revision Time (subjects that are harder to do)

FT = Free Time (sport, hobbies, friends, family etc)

WT = Work Time (job, chores etc)

Now plan your weeks revision in chunks and then **STICK TO IT!**

	Mon	Tues	Weds	Thurs	Fri	Sat	Sun
AM 9am-12	ERT	HRT	ERT	FT	ERT	WT	FT
Afternoon 1pm-3pm	FT	ERT	HRT	HRT	HRT	WT	WT
Afternoon 3pm-	HRT	FT	ERT	ERT	FT	HRT	FT

5pm							
EVE 7pm- 9pm	WT	WT	FT	ERT	WT	FT	FT

Mix your days and weeks up until you find a pattern of structuring your days and weeks that suit you best where you can still relax and have free time for yourself, but also find the time/s when you are at your best for doing the easy revision, as well as the time you are at your very best to tackle the stuff you find scary or difficult as we all know that it is by cracking the hard stuff that our grades will go up.

Far too many students fill their revision time by going over the things they know and understand really well instead of tackling the subject matter that they do not currently understand but they know will be in the exam and could them marks or grades that otherwise they might not achieve.

An author by the name of Scott Alexander wrote an inspiring little book called rhinoceros success in which he describes people as either cows or rhinos. Cows procrastinate and keep putting things off whilst rhinos see what they want and … well… **CHARGE AT THEM !!!!!!!!!**

It is time to release the inner rhino on the things you do not understand and make time to go rhino on these things until you have mastered them.

KEY POINTS FROM CHAPTER 10

1 -   **Work a revision timetable that works**

   for you

2 -   **Allow for free time, easy revision time**

   and HARD revision time

3 -   **Once you have a plan that works...**

   work the plan... stick to it !

4 -   **Go rhino on the harder things!**

Chapter 11 – Memory Skills Make The Difference

There are memory specialists out there that work only on how to get the most of your memory and if this chapter enthuses you I strongly suggest that you check out their work. Tony Buzan, David Thomas, Philip Chambers, to name just three.

As part of my own research I interviewed neuro-scientists who had studied the brains memory and recall systems, memory champions and world mind mapping champions and learnt many varied ways of using the memory to get better recall.

…and yet I found that different people have their own personal favourite, so in this chapter I will "NOT" go deep into how it works and why it works but merely share just two simple, FUN, and easy to apply techniques that have transformed the results and confidence of tens of thousands of students every year for over fifteen years during my talks and workshops in the education sector.

There are many other techniques and I just know that with a little research you will find one that suits you if one of these two do not hit the mark.

For me though, I found these two techniques to really sit well with my own sense of wanting to make learning more "FUN" and they worked for me almost instantly.

Remember the story of Maxtead from earlier in the book who went from a D grade to A* in just four Months? Well, this first technique is the one he used.

Memory Stacking:

Memory stacking is just one of many techniques but one that I find works well for me when remembering lots of information, a plot, story, talk or presentation etc.

I use it for remembering one hour long talks I give or even day long workshops with almost effortless ease.

Without going into the how it works and brain science of it all, you really need to do only a few simple things and make the process as much fun as you can along the way. Your brain likes having fun, so work with it!

To begin with let's say you needed to remember a presentation or a talk. Here are the key messages from a half day workshop that I present in the education sector to students.

You can see that I have kept message brief (in a way that I understand them if I were to read them) and have also highlighted the key word or phrase that would remind me of what it is that I have to remember.

Here are the simple rules to unlocking your recall and memory:

- Know what the message means. It is no good remembering a key word to remind you of a message or formula etc if you then do not understand what that messages is, or what that formula does.
- Do NOT try and remember these things/facts ..... relax and allow your mind to open up (rather than close down when it gets stressed trying to recall things).
- Represent the key things you need to recall with a brightly coloured image.
- Make the image as silly (fun), scary or loving (or sexy) as is appropriate for you to do. These three emotions are very

strong emotions and your mind "adores" them as you easily remember things in your life in the finest of detail where you laughed for ages out loud or had great fun or were at your happiest. You remember with ease the most scary moments of your life, and well... you effortlessly remember the loving or sexy moments eh?

- Stack the images on top of each other in your mind in a silly manner that makes you smile (explained below)
- Have fun effortlessly recalling the images in the stacked order or randomly as required.

For example... to remember to first introduce myself when I am speaking at events, I think of a man wearing a shirt (what ever colour I am wearing that day). I then need to remember to do an icebreaker exercise on assumptions so I think of a large ASS and that image reminds me to do the ASS-umptions exercise.

I then talk about my eighteen years of research and so imagine a large red number eleven. I go on creating a vivid, colourful images that are silly, scary or lovely or sexy, for each of the key points that I need to recall when presenting to a group or audience. Then I have fun in my head stacking these images that represent the information I need to recall on top of each other in a silly way. I might even give these images a silly sound, noise or voice, and so for example, a vampire might talk in a strong Birmingham accent as it makes it easier to recall. The crazier…. The better!

Below you will see a big list of information (my notes showing what I need to say) that I recall as part of a half or full days workshop that I deliver in the education sector. It might mean nothing to you but allow me explain.

* = the explanation of what it means.

Dave - **MAN** in a …**SHIRT**

* I introduce myself to the audience and get rapport with them.
ASSumptions – Live your life based on facts – not assumptions !

* I do an "assumptions" icebreaker exercise

Research Based Development – **18** years of research

* I explain that my work is based upon eighteen years of research
"If you always **D**O what you have always **D**ONE you will always **G**ET what you have always **G**OT"
* I talk about how we have to think and behave differently to get better results.
How good is your memory ? - **Haystack** – try memory stacking for yourself ! (fun, scary or rude)
* a memory exercise that proves they are better than they think they are.
ALMOND NUT *with the word* **YES !!!!!!** *on it* - Almond sized and shaped mass of neurones and electrons within the brain that controls your emotional intelligence. AMYGDALA (Amygdela)

* tell them about the Amygdala and how it controls their emotions.

ANCHOR – *how to change your "state" in a few seconds.*

* get them to do an action that gives them more energy

2   2 – Kriss Akabusi mbe said – "top achievers should be looked **into,** not up **to**!"

who will you look into after today?

* explain the value on having a mentor or coach.

Ralph **Gold** ...

* a story about a successful entrepreneuer

CRAB – cancer research at Birmingham - £288k

* a story about how I have achieved some massive goals

The Massive Goal Principle – **Pyramid**

* the process to set and achieve massive goals

Pavarotti – the singing thing !

* do a singing exercise to show how fear cripples us into non-action.

Comfort Zones (fabric conditioner)

* get them to step out of their comfort zones.

False **Eye**ball (**"I"** DECIDE what I am capable of achieving)

* story about overcoming adversity.

High jumper - The high jump - Raise the bar? – or take it away?

* story about how they should not focus on what they can not do but focus on what they can do.

Think Positive – energy **vampire** with a **Muscled arm**

* an exercise that gets them to experience the power of positive thinking.

USE this information and don't only fill your head with stuff "APPLY IT" - A cup of **WATER**
* a magic trick using a cup of water to show why

we should take action.

And so...

To begin with I would write the list of things that I

need to remember as follows:

Dave - **MAN** in a ...SHIRT

ASSumptions – Live your life based on facts – not assumptions !

Research Based Development – **18** years of

research

"If you always **DO** what you have always **DONE** you will always **GET** what you have always **GOT**"
How good is your memory ?   - **Haystack** – try memory stacking for yourself ! (fun, scary or rude)
ALMOND NUT *with the word* **YES !!!!!!** *on it* -
Almond sized and shaped mass of neurones and electrons within the brain that controls your emotional intelligence. AMYGDALA (Amygdela)

ANCHOR – *how to change your "state" in a few seconds.*

2 **2** – Kriss Akabusi mbe said – "top achievers should be looked **into,** not up **to**!"
who will you look into after today?
Ralph **Gold …**
CRAB – cancer research at Birmingham - £288k
The Massive Goal Principle – **Pyramid**
Pavarotti – the singing thing !
Comfort Zones (fabric conditioner)
False **Eye**ball (**"I"** DECIDE what I am capable of achieving)
High jumper - The high jump - Raise the bar? – or take it away?
Think Positive – energy **vampire** with a **Muscled arm**
USE this information and don't only fill your head with stuff "APPLY IT" - A cup of **WATER.**

I would then grab a few coloured pens or felt tip markers and on a piece of paper or card I would think of a silly, scary or sexy image that (in my mind at least) would help me to recall what I need to talk about.

It is important to say that it matters not if nobody else can make sense of your images as long as you can look at that image and know what it means to you, and what you need to remember. So all that is left to do is have some fun.

It is up to you how you do this but I find it easier to start at the bottom left corner of the page and draw the first image then stack the next one on top of the first one and so on up the page in a zig zag manner as follows.

An example of one of my workshops as a memory stack.
This page might be the only notes I need for a whole days delivery.

Now I would tell myself a silly story that would help to link the images together and aid with recall. As I tell the story I emotionally attatch myself (laugh at silly images, feel shocked at scary images and snigger at rude or sexy images) to the image and sometimes say it out loud including any silly voices that any of the itmes might have been given. Even a solid object that does not speak can easily be remembered if in your mind it is a bright yellow cartoon Egyptian pyramid crying as it sobs…
"I wanted to be a cube!"

My story for the list above would then go something like this.
Picture in your mind a little fat guy from Birmingham wearing a white shirt. When he turns around he has got the biggest ass you have ever seen in your life. With a big red paintbrush you paint the number 18 in red paint onto his ass, and if you look at the number 18, it has the initials DDGG on it in thick blue ink.
On top of the DDGG is a huge yellow haystack and when you look down onto the haystack there is a small almond nut sticking out of the top, and any time you go anywhere near it, the almond nut screams "YES!!!" at you. Hanging off the almond nut is a huge ships anchor and it BANGS (hear a loud bang) into an orange ballerinas tutu (22?).

You put on and wear the orange ballerinas tutu but it is very uncomfortable because sticking out of the side of it is a huge bar of gold. You hear a tapping noise and tapping at the gold bar is a huge red crab and it is pecking at the gold bar with its big red claws, and on the crabs back is a huge Egyptian pyramid.

Look up at the top of your pyramid and standing on the top of the pyramid is a dead opera singer called Pavarotti. Pavarotti opens his mouth to sing but instead he drinks from a bottle of blue comfort fabric conditioner (hear the glugging noise in your head as you imagine him drinking the blue comfort conditioner). On the label of the blue comfort conditioner is a huge false eye ball and see the eye winking at you.

Look into the eye and there is a high jumper jumping over a bar and landing (not on a mattress but) on top of a vampire from Birmingham. The vampire has one large muscular arm and in his hand is a glass of water the he is drinking from.

If you were to go through that story a few times creating the images and emotions and noises as you did so, you would find your recall of the items increasing to astonishing levels. If you were to do one with a list of household items to experiment with the memory stacking process you could have some fun before using it to remember things for your subject revision.

Another example might be that you may need to recall a few facts for History exams about the ancient Romans.

For example, a Roman history revision stack might be like this:
I might need to recall; (in **bold** might be an image I would use to recall them)
The Roman conquest of the world was down to their drill at arms, camp discipline and military expertise.
= A Roman soldier with an arm made from drills (drill at arms) smacking a tent (camp discipline) with a document labelled "expertise" (military expertise).
Shoes – "caligae" leather sandals
= jumping out of the tent is a huge open leather sandal screaming "CALIGAE" loudly.
Mostly fought untrained groups
= the Caligae stamps on a group of crazy Saxons running around in disarray.
Romans stabbed with their sword and did not side swipe
= the last soldier escapes and thrusts/stabs at the Caligae with their sword.
Spear or pilum, would bend upon impact to stop enemy throwing it back
= I would image the Caligae throwing a spear with a purple plum (PiLUM) on the end of a bendy metal spike.

And so… all that information could be recalled by imagining …

An arm made of drill bits, smacking a tent with a document labelled expertise.
Jumping out of the tent is a large open leather sandal screaming "CALIGAE !!".
The Caligae stamps on a group of crazy Saxons in disarray, and the last soldier thrusts or stabs the Caligae with his sword. The Caligae throws a plum javelin at the soldier that has a metal spike which goes all bendy upon impact.
Now you have a go at listing some facts you need to recall for a subject and creating a memory stack of your own.
Next we will look at how best to recall equations, formulae and dates etc that might not be as easy to recall when we are using a memory stack.

Music & Revision Rapping/Rhyming:

When it comes to statistics, dates, names, equations, formula, languages and scripts it can be easier to use music to remember them.

Most people enjoy music and most people have a favourite song or type of music, be it RnB, rap, classical, indie, rock, etc

Feel free to work with your favourite music if you prefer but to start with I would suggest a tune that you know from childhood that is burnt into your memory such as a well known Disney song or nursery rhyme etc.

I have seen many students use rap or hip hop to remember amazing amounts of information and I have even seen an amazing childrens author (Eamonn O'Reilly from the UK) recall all of the key plot lines, characters and themes of a Shakespearian play using a ten minute rap, to a standing ovation from his teenage audience.

The key here is to know the tune and rhythm of the song well. You then replace the lyrics or words of that song with the equation or details you need to recall and make it fit the tune and rhythm of that song.

For example most of us know the flow, tune and rhythm to the famous nursery rhyme "twinkle twinkle little star", and yet we can use that rhyme and tune to recall the following Chemistry facts that in the periodic table the vertical columns are called groups and the horizontal columns are called periods.

"twinkle - twinkle - little - star, how - I - wonder - what - you - are"

upright columns are called groups, ho-ri-zon-tal .... Per-i-ods

And... how about recalling Pi in maths to the tune and rhythm of the American anthem (star spangled banner)

"oh... say, can you see"

"Pie - is three point one four... etc"

Or how about physics ... Albert Einstein's theory of relativity – E=MC2;

(to the tune of the British national anthem).

"God save our gracious queen"

" E   eq-uals M   C squared"

There is also a song by the old British comedy troupe named "Monty Pythons Flying Circus" whose "Galaxy song" is a simple tune that shares dozens of facts about the universe. Well worth a listen.

When trying to recall information in the heat of an exam or test, the brain can seem as if it is shutting down due to the stress or pressure, with many people suggesting that they know the information but simply can not recall it when the pressure is on.

There is much research to suggest that when experiencing stress, emotional or mental tension for any sustained period of time, that the brain is more likely to focus on helping you manage the stress physiologically than remembering things for a test.

One of the best ways to manage the stress is to remove the tension around straining to recall information by making images, tunes, rhymes in your head that are silly and childish and fun as this can help to sabotage the stress and so recall becomes easier.

KEY POINTS FROM CHAPTER 11

1 -   experiment with a memory stack and

        make the images vivid and a little bit

        silly if you can.

2 -   use tunes and music to recall

        equations, formulae and other

        difficult stuff.

Chapter 12 – Revision Buddies / Mastermind Groups

The importance of having somebody to both support you **AND** hold you accountable can never be under-estimated.

I would consider maybe NOT asking your best friend to be that person unless you are both capable of working together without being distracted, and can avoid chatting socially all the time and going onto social media for set periods of time.

Have you heard the expression "you learn best when you teach others"?

Ask a friend to learn something that you struggle with and you learn something that they might not fully understand. Then teach what you have learnt to each other. Teaching others clarifies your understanding or comprehension as well as your recall.

If one of you wants to take time off from the revision schedule, the other person can support you and hold you to account and vice versa.

Two people can make learning fun by playing memory games or making up tunes and singing or rapping them together. Maybe even building in rewards when you achieve a success or a consequence (such as push ups or household chores) when you get things wrong that you maybe should have got right.

Another idea could be to get a small group (mastermind group) together of between three and six people to work on a specific subject that you are lacking in.

Lets us say that you have a small group of fellow students who struggle with maths. Meet up at lunchtime, after school or of an evening or weekend etc.

Take it in turns to share something about the subject that you are struggling with and allow the group to teach those of you who do not understand that thing. Then go round the group taking it in turns to share an issue and getting their subject challenge solved.

If a subject is an issue to the whole of your group, then it would be well worth taking immediate action by maybe going to ask a teacher or subject expert for a little help (as a group) and maybe asking for a lunchtime or after school session on that subject.

Other ideas to resolve a "stuck" situation could include;

- go online and search for the result
- see if anybody has posted a youtube video about it
- go to the library and get out a book on the subject
- post on a forum for help with the subject
- have a competition to see who can find out the answer and understand how to do it first
- go onto teacher forums and ask questions of teachers on that subject

KEY POINTS FROM CHAPTER 12

1 - pick a revision buddy who you know will "work' with you rather than distract you.

2 - get a subject specific mastermind or study group and teach each other the things you do not understand.

3 - go to a teacher as a group to ask for help, if all of you do not understand something.

Chapter 13 – Cards, Sticky Notes, Maps And Audio

If you are reasonably self motivated and have access to some resources such as a local library, paper, pens, sticky notes and some card. Then here are a few great ideas to get the most from your revision.

Mapping:

These things are called many things, most commonly "mind maps" (created by Tony Buzan whose books on memory skills and mind mapping are superb), although often called brain trees or spider diagrams. Go to the local library and ask for books or a DVD on how to mind map, although I bet there are videos online at YouTube at zero cost as well.

It is a fun way of mapping out all the notes you would normally make on many pages of paper, onto one "picture based diagram" that resembles a spiders web. It is not only good fun to create a "mind map" but it still amazes me to this day just how much information can be then recalled simply by picturing your mind map in your head afterwards.

Cards:

Condensing your notes onto hand sized pieces of white or coloured card, and using coloured pens to make your notes can mean you are able to take your revision with you anywhere you go and focus on one item within a subject (one per card) at a time.

You can even turn it into a game where you can't go to the next card in your pile of cards until you have understood and can recall the answer to what is on that card.

Maybe use a different coloured card or coloured pen for each subject or part within each subject?

You can also create yourself a quiz to test yourself using the cards that are easily carried around in your pocket rather than carrying your books around with you all the time.

Use otherwise wasted time to test your knowledge and recall using the cards when sitting on the bus, when the adverts are on Television between programmes , or maybe when sitting on the toilet...... JOKING.... I AM JOKING .... Do NOT use them sitting on the toilet !!! That would be just soooo wrong on every level okay?!

Sticky notes:

A similar concept to the cards (above) but if you get support from your family you can stick them around the house, maybe even a subject in each room or part of a room, and you can move around the house looking at your notes challenging yourself, or asking your family to challenge you to recall the facts or information.

Post the difficult ones in the toilet maybe or even on the wall as you go up the stairs and you are not allowed to leave the toilet or go up or down stairs until you have answered the question or recalled the fact etc.

"Seriously though…. I do not expect you to lock yourself in the toilet okay !?"

The good thing about the sticky notes is that they will not get lost as they stick to the wall, and they easily peel off without leaving any marks.

You can write questions on one note and the answers on another coloured note, then put all the question notes neatly at one end of a wall or table and try to place the answer notes with the correct question notes.

Audio

If you have a language, script or poem to learn, recording yourself on your phone using audio recording can mean you can listen to yourself, making sure that you get the words right. Maybe learn a language by singing your favourite songs in the language you are learning, or maybe get yourself a pen pal online from that country (who may also wish to learn English from you?) and each of you talking to the other person... ONLY in their respective languages.

Audio recording your key facts to recall can also then be downloaded onto your phone or ipod etc listen to as you walk, cycle etc to embed your learning and recall.

There has been much written (and made up) about the value of having music on in the background whilst learning. Some say that they work best with Metallica blasting out or Beyonce pounding the speakers or headphones, but "most" of the top achievers I have asked about this have said they get their best results from having music that has no words or lyrics to them, that are around 60 bpm (beats per minute), and is quietly playing at a barely audible level in the background. Classical baroque (yeah... even if you don't like classical it is worth a try eh?) is said to be very good and certainly helped me when I was revising using these techniques.

So ditch the loud music when learning and try "Classic FM" radio station instead, if only for the revision times.

The theory here is that the music is heard by the creative side of your brain leaving the logical side of the brain open to learn and receive information without being distracted by the creative mind saying things to you such as "must be time for a coffee?", or "I will just message my mates", or "what a nice view out the window" etc.

Also, do revisit the section on memory as I have used music to recall LOADS of information that way.

KEY POINTS FROM CHAPTER 13

1 - Use your favourite music, rhymes or songs to help anchor information in your mind and effortlessly recall that information by having fun.

2 - learn how to use mind maps to condense huge amounts of information into a one page picture.

3 - use hand held cards as revision aids, recall prompts or quiz cards.

4 - cover the house with sticky post-it notes and use your whole house as a learning zone.

Chapter 14 – Looking After Number One

… (eat, sleep and drink wisely)

It is time to get a little selfish …. But in a good way.

There is much conflicting evidence around what is good and what is not so good for us when studying.

They used to say drink lots of water and they seems now to say that too much water can dilute the impact of essential vitamins and bacteria etc

So what should we believe?

I am no scientist but I do believe that we are all different, and some of us use that as an excuse to say that "drinking energy drinks works for me" when I can find zero testimony to that other than the initial ten to fifteen minute hit of caffeine you get.

Sadly that high is too quickly followed by lethargy and tiredness as our body works hard to cope with the sugar and caffeine that has been pumped into it.

Sure … have a treat, but much of the time it is down to common sense.

Even if you only look after yourself for your revision and exam periods, (and I of course suggest that it is longer term …..) it surely must be worth doing this to get the most from the miracle of bio-engineering that is your body.

- Chose water for nearly all of your liquid intake every day
- Try to take one to two litres of water in addition to any other drinks
- **Avoid drinks high in sugar, caffeine, flavouring and additives**

I am the first to admit that the lure of fast food, and foods that are "less than good" for us can at times be just too much to resist. However, to get the best out of your brain I would suggest a "NO GO ZONE" on such foods during revision, learning and exam periods.

Again try to avoid foods with too much salt, sugar or additives in them and focus your intake on fresh, natural foods. Current thinking suggests that oily fish such as mackerel, salmon, sardines contain high levels of Omega three oils which are said to help the brain with learning, retention and recall.

Maybe take a vitamin tablet, or try other small efforts to make you healthier whilst you embark upon the most critical part of your life.

There is little wrong with giving yourself a treat every now and then if you have learnt or recalled some great information that was previously defeating you but for "most" of your food intake focus on fresh foods and natural foods.

- Select a balanced intake of protein, carbohydrates and fresh vegetables and fruit.

- Try eating smaller and more frequent meals to maintain sugar levels, focus and energy levels.
- **Avoid high salt, sugar and saturated fat rich food that can impair energy, focus and cause weight gain... as I know all too well myself.**

There are many studies that highlight concern over sleep patterns of young adults due to pressure from peers to stay online chatting or gaming late into the night.

For others it may be stress, family or other emotional issues that can cause sleep loss, however the effect on the brain of long term sleep loss (especially in young adults) can play havoc with learning and recall during revision and exam periods.

I know you may love staying up late, or you might consider it "lame" or "boring" to go to bed early but during these periods you really do owe it to yourself to give sleep a chance to give you every opportunity of being at your very best to get the grades you deserve.

If you are not tired, make sure that you build into each day some fresh air, exercise and stretching. Try relaxation techniques, counting sheep in your head, or deep breathing or even meditation.… Anything to hep you to get to sleep.

I will not tell you how many hours sleep you need as it can vary from individual to individual, however the brain and body of a young adult tends to need more, rather than less sleep.

The fact that young people can cope with less sleep better than older people can mean that the effects can not so easily be spotted, but many of the school teachers I work with can report that when sleep deprived students get consistent good nights sleep that their attitude, behaviour, retention, recall and RESULTS improve.

Do accept that this is in no way a challenge that is intended to stop you having fun, having tasty treats, the odd late night etc, but more a call to action for a short period of time (starting BEFORE the exam period as it can take a few days of getting good quality sleep to get the full benefit of this) in the hope that the benefits you receive will encourage you to do more of it post exams.

KEY POINTS FROM CHAPTER 14

1 -   get some good quality sleep in both

the run up to, and during revision

and exam periods.

2 -   stay hydrated, replacing energy drinks

with water.

3 -   avoid heavily processed foods and

maybe even consider taking

advice from a doctor on vitamins and

minerals.

Chapter 15 – Environment

Where do you learn best?

Consider the following sample list of environments and circle or note the ones which you think are the ones where you are able to work your best. Then consider finding such a place that ticks most of your preferences and dedicate most of your learning and revision time to working in this area.

School, home or Library?

Online, offline, written, audio or video?

Kitchen table or Bedroom etc?

Outside or Inside?

Quiet area, low background noise or maybe a Noisy area?

Warm, tepid or cool temperature?

Window and door open, closed, or slightly open?

Darker room, brightly lit room, or average lighting?

Natural light, or fluorescent lighting?

Sat down, stood up, or moving around?

Hard chair, comfy chair or bean bag?

How many others can you think of?

Phone on, phone off, or agreed times when you play on the phone?

Music on, music off, or agreed times to play music?

Computer, pens and paper, or practical "doing" learning?

On your own, with a revision buddy or team, or a mixture of both?

Television on, TV off, or on in another room as background noise?

Morning, afternoon, or evening revision?

Work 20 minutes at a time, 40 minutes at a time, or an hour at a time?

Do what works best for you if you can make that happen. Serve yourself by giving yourself every chance of success by ensuring that your learning environment is as suitable to your personal needs as possible.

Set up your revision zone, and dedicate yourself to use it most of the time that you are able to do so.

Help yourself, to help yourself, by being ready to learn. Ensure you have paper, pens etc.

Here is a little list to help you get started.

Pens and pencils

Felt tip pens or coloured pencils

Paper

Coloured card

Sticky note pads

Laptop or computer (or booked time on a computer at a library or internet cafe)

Mobile phone or other audio recording device

Past papers

Drinking water

Healthy energy snacks

KEY POINTS FROM CHAPTER 15

1 -   know what environment suits your

        learning best.

2 -   set your learning zone up to best serve

        you … and USE IT !

Chapter 16 – Past Papers

Yes ….. I know …. Teachers bang on about using past papers all the time eh?

Ask yourself why they do that?

From year to year exam boards use similar and at times identical questions from the previous and recent years exams and so to put it simply, doing past papers is the very best way to see how much you know, understand, can recall, and it will also test your ability to read exam questions and answer the questions and get feedback from your teacher or lecturer in advance of your exams.

It is also a superb opportunity to see how well you read exam papers.

What do I mean by this?

(sharp intake of breath)

I am not proud of this but teachers always say "READ THE QUESTION FIRST".

When I was in high school I was only really good at two subjects, English and Geography. I entered these exams with at least a hope of doing okay because I thought I knew it well because I liked the subjects.

I opened the exam paper and thought at once that there was no way I would be able to answer all ten "quite detailed" questions in the time allotted for the exam. Panic flooded my mind and I raced through most of the questions half answering each one in the hope of doing "okay".

The next day in lessons I was shocked to hear that I should have read the paper first as it "CLEARLY" stated (although I did not see this) that I only needed to answer four of the ten questions.

FOUR OF THE TEN QUESTIONS !!!! …… I was NOT a happy man.

It was of course my own fault for not reading the question properly.

Make sure that you read the paper well.

KEY POINTS FROM CHAPTER 16

1 -   Get past papers from recent years

2 -   practise reading the questions

3 -   get quality feedback on your answers

       to the exam paper questions

Chapter 17 – Ask For Help

This may be near the end of the book but I can't stress enough how important this chapter is. It can be the game changer for you.

When we are young, many of us can tend to be scared of asking for help for one or more of many reasons. Maybe we are scared of ridicule for not knowing the answer. Maybe we fear being critisized by the teacher or lecturer for "not listening" first time it was explained. There are many other reasons.

Do you think the worlds greatest sports people have a coach?

Top golfers, for example, will have different coaches for every part of their game. One for putting, one for driving, one for fairway etc.

So… if the best of the best can ask for help….
Why would anyone of any quality or substance
think that asking for help is a sign of weakness?
It just does not make sense does it?

Frequently the part of a subject that we are stuck
on can mean valuable marks are being lost in
the exam simply out of a meaningless fear of
asking for help beforehand.

My simple, short and sincere advice to you here
is to list the things that you know or have been
told will or might be in your exams that you
currently struggle with, and go out there and find
someone to help you understand it.

Whilst your time, energy, resources and
motivation are at their peak, go and learn the
hard stuff first. This way, instead of your revision
getting harder, it will appear to get easier for you.

KEY POINTS FROM CHAPTER 17

1 -   **List the subject areas you struggle**

         with

2 -   **ASK FOR HELP … NOW !**

Chapter 18 – Your Learning Style

There are many online profiling tools and questionnaires that can help you to understand your preferred learning style however we are all capable of learning in many ways and styles.

Some of us are naturally better at reading and writing.

An example of this being the use of a text book and writing notes when revising.

Others of us prefer to watch a subject being taught either live or on video.

By this I of course mean a class, lecture or video.

Then others prefer to do an activity that explains the subject.

Learning to play the piano is first explained then you straight away go and sit at a piano and start to play the thing … even if it is badly at first.

When it comes to something like revising a chemical equation or formula, you could:

a) Read about it in a text book and write it out and learn it this way.

b) Watch a video of a cartoon character explaining the formula or maybe going to a class or lecture to watch somebody draw it out for you before you have a go yourself.

c) Create a rhyme or rap to remember the formula and how to use it whilst dancing around the room.

There should be no wrong way of learning a subject if it works for you

KEY POINTS FROM CHAPTER 18

1 -   Re-read this page and consider how

        best you learn... and make most of

        your revision fit your preferred style.

Conclusion:

We can dream of what we want to achieve, hoping that we get a result we want through luck, or we can go and get what we want by taking the right action and improving our effectiveness in how we learn and revise.

We can dismiss new information and ways of thinking as silly, strange or simplistic, or we can try them out to see if they have any positive impact, and if (or when) they do, use them in our toolkit of strategies to help us towards our goals.

We can pretend that we are not bothered about exam results or learning, although behind the apathy lies only fear of the unknown or lack of ability, or we can have a go, learn what went wrong if we slip up first time around, and come back fighting determined more than ever to succeed.

And at the blow of the final whistle, should the result not meet our expectation or need, we can hang our head with disappointment, and limp off into the sunset licking our wounds, or we can stand up, brush ourselves down, steel our resolve and retake the exam screaming at the top of our lungs

"IS THAT ALL YOU'VE GOT...... REALLY !?"

Or...

We can change our attitude for the better, behaving and acting every moment of every day as if we were the successful person that we deserve to be.

We can accept that things may not go our way, and that we can also learn from stumbles, trips and falls.

We can help others to succeed as it has been said that we learn best when we teach others.

We can be in it for the long game, knowing with certainty that one day we shall taste the sweetness of victory.

We can chose to believe in ourselves knowing that we are not made of glass and a mistake will not cause injury or death.

We can chose our response when those around us tell us that we "can't", are not "able" or clever enough, and instead of wilting, raise our face towards the sun and shine.

Success is yours to own if you act.

So... ACT !

I wish you every success in your learning and revision journey and pray that you get all that you deserve through having done all that is required of you. Be good … or better.

David Hyner

Printed in Great Britain
by Amazon

64405968R00113